# THE SEVEN CHURCHES OF REVELATION
### STUDY GUIDE

DAVID JEREMIAH

**with Dr. David Jeremiah**

© 2016 Turning Point for God
P.O. Box 3838
San Diego, CA 92163
All Rights Reserved

Revised by: William Kruidenier
Unless otherwise indicated, Scripture verses quoted are from the NEW KING JAMES VERSION.

Printed in the United States of America.

# Contents

About Dr. David Jeremiah and Turning Point . . . . . 4

About This Study Guide . . . . . . . . . . . . . . . . . . . . . . . 5

Introduction . . . . . . . . . . . . . . . . . . . . . . . . . . . . . . . . . 7

1. Christ in the Midst of His Churches
   *Revelation 1:9-20* . . . . . . . . . . . . . . . . . . . . . . . . 9

2. Losing Your First Love:
   The Letter to the Church in Ephesus
   *Revelation 2:1-7* . . . . . . . . . . . . . . . . . . . . . . . 21

3. The Suffering Church:
   The Letter to the Church in Smyrna
   *Revelation 2:8-11* . . . . . . . . . . . . . . . . . . . . . . 35

4. The Church of Satan's City:
   The Letter to the Church in Pergamos
   *Revelation 2:12-17* . . . . . . . . . . . . . . . . . . . . . 47

5. The Adulterous Church:
   The Letter to the Church in Thyatira
   *Revelation 2:18-29* . . . . . . . . . . . . . . . . . . . . . 59

6. The Dead Church:
   The Letter to the Church in Sardis
   *Revelation 3:1-6* . . . . . . . . . . . . . . . . . . . . . . . 71

7. The Faithful Church:
   The Letter to the Church in Philadelphia
   *Revelation 3:7-13* . . . . . . . . . . . . . . . . . . . . . . 87

8. The Disgusting Church:
   The Letter to the Church in Laodicea
   *Revelation 3:14-22* . . . . . . . . . . . . . . . . . . . . . 99

9. A Look Into Heaven
   *Revelation 4:1-11* . . . . . . . . . . . . . . . . . . . . . 113

Resources . . . . . . . . . . . . . . . . . . . . . . . . . . . . . . . . 126

Stay Connected . . . . . . . . . . . . . . . . . . . . . . . . . . . . 128

# About Dr. David Jeremiah and Turning Point

Dr. David Jeremiah is the founder of Turning Point, a ministry committed to providing Christians with sound Bible teaching relevant to today's changing times through radio and television broadcasts, audio series, books, and live events. Dr. Jeremiah's common-sense teaching on topics such as family, prayer, worship, angels, and biblical prophecy forms the foundation of Turning Point.

David and his wife, Donna, reside in El Cajon, California, where he serves as the senior pastor of Shadow Mountain Community Church. David and Donna have four children and twelve grandchildren.

In 1982, Dr. Jeremiah brought the same solid teaching to San Diego television that he shares weekly with his congregation. Shortly thereafter, Turning Point expanded its ministry to radio. Dr. Jeremiah's inspiring messages can now be heard worldwide on radio, television, and the Internet.

Because Dr. Jeremiah desires to know his listening audience, he travels nationwide holding ministry rallies and spiritual enrichment conferences that touch the hearts and lives of many people. According to Dr. Jeremiah, "At some point in time, everyone reaches a turning point; and for every person, that moment is unique, an experience to hold onto forever. There's so much changing in today's world that sometimes it's difficult to choose the right path. Turning Point offers people an understanding of God's Word as well as the opportunity to make a difference in their lives."

Dr. Jeremiah has authored numerous books, including *Escape the Coming Night* (Revelation), *The Handwriting on the Wall* (Daniel), *Overcoming Loneliness, Prayer—The Great Adventure, God in You* (Holy Spirit), *When Your World Falls Apart, Slaying the Giants in Your Life, My Heart's Desire, Sanctuary, Captured by Grace, Signs of Life, What in the World Is Going On?, The Coming Economic Armageddon, I Never Thought I'd See the Day!, God Loves You: He Always Has—He Always Will, What Are You Afraid Of?,* and *Agents of the Apocalypse.*

# About This Study Guide

The purpose of this Turning Point study guide is to reinforce Dr. David Jeremiah's dynamic, in-depth teaching and to aid the reader in applying biblical truth to his or her daily life. This study guide is designed to be used in conjunction with Dr. Jeremiah's *The Seven Churches of Revelation* audio series, but it may also be used by itself for personal or group study.

## Structure of the Lessons

Each lesson is based on one of the messages in the *The Seven Churches of Revelation* compact disc series and focuses on specific passages in the Bible. Each lesson is composed of the following elements:

- *Outline*

The outline at the beginning of the lesson gives a clear, concise picture of the topic being studied and provides a helpful framework for readers as they listen to Dr. Jeremiah's teaching.

- *Overview*

The overview summarizes Dr. Jeremiah's teaching on the passage being studied in the lesson. Readers should refer to the Scripture passages in their own Bibles as they study the overview. Unless otherwise indicated, Scripture verses quoted are taken from the New King James Version.

- *Application*

This section contains a variety of questions designed to help readers dig deeper into the lesson and the Scriptures, and to apply the lesson to their daily lives. For Bible study groups or Sunday school classes, these questions will provide a springboard for group discussion and interaction.

- *Did You Know?*

This section presents a fascinating fact, historical note, or insight that adds a point of interest to the preceding lesson.

# Using This Guide for Group Study

The lessons in this study guide are suitable for Sunday school classes, small-group studies, elective Bible studies, or home Bible study groups. Each person in the group should have his or her own study guide.

When possible, the study guide should be used with the corresponding compact disc series. You may wish to assign the study guide lesson as homework prior to the meeting of the group and then use the meeting time to listen to the CD and discuss the lesson.

# For Continuing Study

For a complete listing of Dr. Jeremiah's materials for personal and group study call 1-800-947-1993, go online to www.DavidJeremiah.org, or write to: Turning Point, P.O. Box 3838, San Diego, CA 92163.

Dr. Jeremiah's *Turning Point* program is currently heard or viewed around the world on radio, television, and the Internet in English. *Momento Decisivo*, the Spanish translation of Dr. Jeremiah's messages, can be heard on radio in every Spanish speaking country in the world. The television broadcast is also broadcast by satellite throughout the Middle East with Arabic subtitles.

Contact Turning Point for radio and television program times and stations in your area. Or visit our website at www.DavidJeremiah.org.

# The Seven Churches of Revelation

## INTRODUCTION

The first step in Bible study is always to determine what the passage of Scripture meant originally. Who wrote it, when and why, and to whom? Scholars refer to this as the grammatical-historical step—determining what the Bible meant in its original context. We could also call it discovering the *primary* meaning.

But there is a second step: What does the Scripture passage mean to me? Obviously, we in the twenty-first century are not the Bible's original recipients. So how do we take what was written for others and find application for our life? We could refer to this as discovering the personal meaning of a text.

We could apply those two steps—*primary* interpretation and *personal* application—and be well equipped for the task of "rightly dividing the word of truth" (2 Timothy 2:15).

But there is a third dimension to Bible study that sometimes needs to be discovered: the *prophetic* perspective. All passages have a *primary* interpretation and a *personal* application, but some also have a *prophetic* application. That means they have a general relevance that reaches beyond the primary (the past) and the personal (the present) and extends into the future. Christ's messages to seven first-century churches in Asia Minor require all three kinds of understanding: *primary*, *personal*, and *prophetic*.

Christ gave these messages to the apostle John during his exile on the island of Patmos. Sent there by a Roman emperor to lessen his influence on the growth of Christian churches in the Empire, John received a revelation from Jesus Christ about "the things which you have seen, and the things which are, and the things which will take place after this" (Revelation 1:19).

The "things which you have seen" are the revelation of Christ Himself to John in chapter one. The "things which are" constitute the seven messages of Christ to seven churches in Asia Minor—churches in the cities of Ephesus, Smyrna, Pergamum, Thyatira, Sardis, Philadelphia, and Laodicea. These messages are found in Revelation 2-3. The "things which will take place after this" make up the rest of the book: Revelation 4-22.

The primary focus of this study guide, *The Seven Churches of Revelation,* is the phrase "the things which are." This study guide has nine chapters: an introductory chapter dealing with John's vision of Christ, seven chapters covering each of Christ's letters to the seven churches, and a final letter of John's introductory vision of heaven in Revelation 4.

In the seven lessons covering the seven letters to the churches, all three levels of Bible study are employed. The *primary* perspective covers the historical setting of each church in the first century. The *personal* perspective draws out application for personal and church life today. And most uniquely, the *prophetic* perspective reveals how these seven churches have remarkable similarity to seven successive periods of church history—from the first century to the twenty-first century.

For example, following the order of the churches as addressed by Christ, the church in Ephesus represents the first-century apostolic Church; the church in Smyrna represents the persecuted Church of the second and third centuries; the church in Pergamum represents the worldly Church after it was co-opted by the Roman Emperor Constantine; the church in Thyatira is like the Church during the Middle Ages; the church in Sardis bears striking resemblance to the Church of the Protestant Reformation; the church in Philadelphia reminds us of the Church in the modern missionary movement; and the church in Laodicea represents the apostate Church at the end of this age.

This journey through Revelation 1-4 will deepen your devotion to Christ, provide you with lessons and warnings about the local church, and pull back the curtain on the glory of heaven in the throne room of God.

# LESSON 1

# CHRIST IN THE MIDST OF HIS CHURCHES

*Revelation 1:9-20*

*In this lesson we discover the only biblical description of the physical appearance of Jesus Christ.*

### OUTLINE

Everyone has seen artists' renditions of the first-century Jesus of Nazareth. As appealing as they might be, Scripture doesn't say what Jesus looked like until we get to the Bible's last book. In Revelation, the apostle John describes the Jesus who will come again as King and Judge of all.

I. **This Vision Was Seen by John While in Exile on the Isle of Patmos**

II. **This Vision Was Received by John While in the Spirit on the Lord's Day**

III. **This Vision Was to Be Written by John and Sent to the Seven Churches**

IV. **This Vision Is of the Glorified, Risen Son of Man**
   A. The Position of Christ in the Vision
   B. The Portrait of Christ in the Vision

V. **The Vision Paralyzed John Until He Was Touched by the Lord**
   A. Fear Not for I Am the Eternal God
   B. Fear Not for I Am the Resurrected Christ
   C. Fear Not for I Have the Keys of Death and Hell

## OVERVIEW

If you have ever wondered what Jesus of Nazareth looked like, you are not alone. It's perfectly normal to think about how He appeared. But, biblically speaking, we don't know. The Bible makes only one reference to Jesus' appearance and even it was not made by an eyewitness. When prophesying about the coming Messiah, Isaiah wrote, "He has no form or comeliness; and when we see Him, there is no beauty that we should desire Him" (Isaiah 53:2). In other words, there was apparently nothing striking or unusual about Jesus' physical appearance. He likely would have blended into a crowd of everyday Jews of His day.

We do, however, have a very detailed description of Jesus' glorified appearance—how He looked after He ascended to heaven. Revelation 1 gives us a view not of the lowly Galilean carpenter but the lofty glorified Christ who appeared to the apostle John on the island of Patmos off the coast of Asia Minor (modern Turkey). This is the Christ who will come in His glory to judge all the earth. He appeared to John in all His ascended glory to convey "the things which are, and the things which will take place" (Revelation 1:19).

# THIS VISION WAS SEEN BY JOHN WHILE IN EXILE ON THE ISLE OF PATMOS (REVELATION 1:9)

Many Bible books were written under great duress. Moses wrote the Pentateuch in the wilderness. David wrote many psalms while being persecuted by Saul. Jeremiah was severely persecuted in Jerusalem. Peter wrote his two letters just prior to his martyrdom. And Paul, of course, wrote four letters while in jail in Rome and his final letter to Timothy while in prison just before being martyred. Paul's whole life as an apostle was spent under great duress, during which he wrote all of his letters (2 Corinthians 11:24-28).

Now we find the apostle John in exile on the tiny, rocky island of Patmos. He was sent there by the Romans to reduce his religious influence in the Roman Empire. Exile, for the Romans, was a death sentence. It was a horrible existence. Yet it was in such a setting that John received the revelation from Christ that we now call the book of Revelation—the most detailed vision of things to come given to any apostle.

John had been the leader, the overseer, of the churches in Asia Minor. He was sent there "for" (on account of) his preaching and testimony for Christ (verse 9). If the apostle whom Jesus loved (John 20:2; 21:7, 20) was allowed to undergo such severe testing, should we be surprised if we likewise are tested? Paul wrote that "we also glory in tribulation" because it leads to perseverance, character, and hope (Romans 5:3-5). And Jesus said that "in the world [we] will have tribulation." But we know that He has overcome the world (John 16:33).

Note three words in Revelation 1:9: tribulation, kingdom, and patience. Those words are a paradigm for our lives as Christians. We live between the realities of kingdom life and tribulation in this world—and that calls for patience. When we experience victory, we are surprised by tribulation. And when we experience trouble, we long for victory. Patience is the link between those two. Patience is what allows us to endure between present reality and future hope.

# THIS VISION WAS RECEIVED BY JOHN WHILE IN THE SPIRIT ON THE LORD'S DAY (REVELATION 1:10)

Christ appeared to John on Patmos while he was "in the Spirit on the Lord's Day." John uses the phrase "in the Spirit" three other times in Revelation: 4:2; 17:3; 21:10. In those situations John was in a spiritual realm, beyond the confines of his bodily limitations and senses in order to receive something not otherwise perceptible.

The "Lord's Day" is probably not a reference to the first day of the Jewish week (our Sunday), but the Day of the Lord—the "time of Jacob's trouble" (Jeremiah 30:7), the coming Tribulation of which he was about to see visions. He was "fast forwarded" into the future to see what is yet to come upon the earth.

# THIS VISION WAS TO BE WRITTEN BY JOHN AND SENT TO THE SEVEN CHURCHES (REVELATION 1:11-12)

John looked and saw "seven golden lampstands" (verse 12) that represented the seven churches Christ mentioned in verse 11 (see verse 20). John is to write to these seven churches. Standing amidst the seven lampstands was "One like the Son of Man" (verse 13). Jesus came as "the light of the world" (John 1:9; 8:12) and then commissioned us to be "the light of the world" (Matthew 5:14).

Thus the Church (the churches in this world) are to be like lampstands shining forth Christ's light in a dark world. The Church (a lampstand) is not the light; Christ is the light. The purpose of the lampstand (the Church) is to bear the light of Christ in the world.

John's first vision was of Christ standing in the midst of seven lampstands representing seven churches in Asia Minor.

# THIS VISION IS OF THE GLORIFIED, RISEN SON OF MAN (REVELATION 1:13-16)

John begins to describe the "Son of Man" standing in the midst of the lampstands.

### *The Position of Christ in the Vision (Revelation 1:13)*

We can imagine the seven lampstands arranged in a circle with Christ standing in the middle (see Revelation 2:1 and Matthew 18:20). Jesus Christ's appropriate place is to be the central focus of His Church. In too many churches today, He is not.

### *The Portrait of Christ in the Vision (Revelation 1:13-16)*

Seven aspects of Christ's appearance are given in detail.

1. His Clothing (verse 13)

Christ was clothed "with a garment down to the feet and girded about the chest with a golden band." Such a robe and belt speaks of greatness (Isaiah 6:1; 11:5).

2. His Head and Hair (verse 14a)

His head and hair were "white like wool, as white as snow." White was the color of age, wisdom, and dignity befitting a judge. It is the same picture Daniel saw of the Ancient of Days whose hair "was like pure wool" (Daniel 7:9).

3. His Eyes (verse 14b)

Christ's eyes were "like a flame of fire." John had seen Jesus' eyes in lots of different situations, but here they are the penetrating eyes of fire—eyes from whom nothing is hidden, eyes that will judge all mankind (Psalm 11:4; Hebrews 4:13).

4. His Feet (verse 15a)

His feet "were like fine brass," a symbol of judgment in Scripture. His feet being of brass means that Christ will one day put all evil and all enemies under His feet.

5. His Mouth (verse 15b; 16b)

There are two dimensions to Christ's mouth: the sound and the sword. The sound of His voice was like "the sound of many waters." Coming out of His mouth was "a sharp two-edged sword".

This sound was the same sound Ezekiel heard when God spoke (Ezekiel 43:2; see also Psalm 93:4). Think of the roar of Niagara Falls or any other great waterfall; it drowns out all other conversations. When Christ returns, His voice of judgment will be the only voice heard.

The sword is the Word of God (Ephesians 6:17). When Christ returns, it will be His Word that slays His enemies (Revelation 2:16; 19:15a, 21).

6. His Hands (verse 16a)

In His right hand Christ held "seven stars," a picture of the authority that has been given by the Father to the Son (Matthew 28:18). The right hand is the place of authority (Ephesians 1:20). I believe the stars stand for the pastors of the seven churches who stand in a place of authority as representatives of Christ in their churches—not *their* authority, but *Christ's* authority. Daniel saw "those who turn many to righteousness" as being "like the stars forever and ever" (Daniel 12:3).

7. His Face (verse 16b)

Jesus' "countenance was like the sun shining in its strength." John had seen the face of Jesus on the Mount of Transfiguration where Jesus' face "shone like the sun" (Matthew 17:2). Perhaps what he saw on Patmos was similar. It may be the same brightness that Paul saw when Christ encountered him on the road to Damascus—a light "brighter than the sun" (Acts 26:13). Taken together, the images represent nothing less than the glory of the risen Christ.

# THE VISION PARALYZED JOHN UNTIL HE WAS TOUCHED BY THE LORD (REVELATION 1:17)

How would you respond if suddenly confronted by what John saw? Probably the same way John responded! He "fell at [Christ's] feet as dead." This is not an unusual response when people are in the presence of God. Abraham fell on his face (Genesis 17:3); Moses hid his face (Exodus 3:6); Balaam fell on his face (Numbers 22:31); Joshua fell on his face (Joshua 5:14); Gideon thought he was going to die (Judges 6:22-23) . . . and on and on. It is apparently a terrifying thing to find oneself in the presence of pure holiness and righteousness.

Jesus' touch and words of comfort were enough to revive the apostle. While John was lying prostrate at Jesus' feet, Jesus reached out and laid His right hand on John with a touch of assurance. And He said to John, "Do not be afraid." Immediately following these initial words of comfort, Jesus gave John three reasons not to be afraid—words that can keep us from being afraid as well.

## *Fear Not for I Am the Eternal God (Revelation 1:17)*

The first reason is because Christ is the eternal God: "I am the First and the Last." If Christ is the first, there was none before Him. If He is the last, there will be none after Him. "I am" calls to mind the name of God given to Moses in Exodus 3:14. And "the First and the Last" parallels His names as "the Alpha and the Omega," the first and last letters of the Greek alphabet (Revelation 21:6).

If Christ is the First and the Last then there is no one with His eternality and authority. There is no one and nothing that can separate us from Him (Romans 8:35-39).

## *Fear Not for I Am the Resurrected Christ (Revelation 1:18a)*

The second reason John needed not to be afraid is because the One speaking to him was the resurrected Lord Jesus Christ: "I am He who lives, and was dead, and behold, I am alive forevermore. Amen."

Peter wrote that we have "a living hope through the resurrection of Jesus Christ from the dead" (1 Peter 1:3). Christ says He is the One "who lives" (present tense) in spite of having been "dead"— and now He is "alive forevermore" never to die again. The same thing will be true for any and all who put their faith in Him: "He who believes in Me, though he may die, he shall live. And whoever lives and believes in Me shall never die" (John 11:25-26). The same eternal life that Christ enjoys is the eternal life those who trust in Him will enjoy.

Death is the one thing human beings fear most. The writer of the letter to the Hebrews says that those who fear death are "all their lifetime subject to bondage" (Hebrews 2:15). But Christ has come to release us from that fear.

The apostle John probably thought he was going to die on the island of Patmos. But Christ reached out and touched John and assured him that He is the eternal One who lives forevermore. What can we possibly fear in life if the resurrected Christ promises us deliverance from death and the promise of eternal life?

## *Fear Not for I Have the Keys of Death and Hell (Revelation 1:18b)*

The third reason John shouldn't have been afraid was because Christ has "the keys of Hades and of Death." Not only does Christ have power over death, He also has power over the grave. These are parallel ways of saying the same thing, of course. If one has power over death, that power extends to the grave. John, who likely saw Patmos as his own grave, was being reminded by Christ that the grave is not the end of the story. There is another chapter written on the other side of the grave, and Christ is the author of that text.

We live in a day when portraits of Jesus Christ are plentiful. Some are respectfully composed by artists, but others are cartoonish caricatures offered up by late-night comedians. Many in the modern world degrade Christ, His ministry, and all that is done in His name. Even though we don't know what the first-century Jesus looked like, we know He is history's most beautiful person, worthy of honor and glory.

Those who have mocked His beauty will one day stand before Him as the apostle Paul wrote: "at the name of Jesus every knee should bow, in heaven and on earth and under the earth" (Philippians 2:10; see also Isaiah 45:23; Romans 14:11). And we know what that Jesus will look like—He will look like the Jesus that appeared to John the apostle on Patmos! And when the world sees Him for who He is, its response will be the same as John's—to fall prostrate at His feet.

We have a choice as to how we see Him and fall before Him. We can fall in holy fear (honor and awe) or human fear. If we belong to Him by faith, we will fall at His feet in worship and adoration for who He is and what He has done. If we do not belong to Him we will fall in fear for our lives; we will shrink back when we hear the thunder of His voice, see the fire in His eyes, and understand the meaning of the sword in His mouth. The choice is ours to make—today.

In his book on fear, pastor and author Max Lucado wrote the following:

We fear being sued, finishing last, going broke; we fear the mole on the back, the new kid on the block, the sound of the clock as it ticks us closer to the grave. We sophisticate investment plans, create elaborate security systems, and legislate stronger military, yet we depend on mood-altering drugs more than any other generation in history. Moreover, "ordinary children today are more fearful than psychiatric patients were in the 1950s…"

Fear herds us into a prison and slams the doors.

Wouldn't it be great to walk out?

This is Jesus' desire for you. His most common command emerges from the "fear not" genre. The Gospels list some 125 Christ-issued imperatives. Of these, 21 urge us "not to be afraid" or "have courage" or "take heart." The second most common command, to love God and neighbor appears on only eight occasions. If quantity is any indicator, Jesus takes our fears seriously. The one statement he made more than any other was this: don't be afraid.

Imagine your life untouched by angst. What if faith, not fear was your default reaction to threats? Envision a day, just one day, absent the dread of failure, rejection, and calamity. Can you imagine a life with no fear?

Fear may fill our world, but it doesn't have to fill our hearts. It will always knock on the door. Just don't invite it in for dinner. Let's embolden our heart with a select number of Jesus' "do not fear" statements. The promise of Christ is simple: we can fear less tomorrow than we can today.[1]

If you had been John on the island of Patmos, how would you have responded when Jesus appeared in all His glory? After the shock of seeing Him, would you have worshiped Him or cowered in fear for having ignored Him in your life? Jesus' words to John are His words to you today: "Do not be afraid; I am the First and the Last. I am He who lives, and was dead, and behold, I am alive forevermore. Amen. And I have the keys of Hades and of Death."

As we begin this series of lessons on *The Seven Churches of Revelation*, make sure you have taken Jesus' words to heart.

Notes:

1. Max Lucado, *Fearless: Imagine Your Life Without Fear* (Nashville, TN: Thomas Nelson, 2009), 5-6, 10, 13.

## APPLICATION

1. How did Isaiah the prophet describe the Suffering Servant (Messiah) who was to come? (Isaiah 53:2)

   a. In what sense might Jesus have appeared as an "average" Jewish man of His day?

   b. How does Isaiah's description of the Servant in verse 2 fit the description of Him in the immediate context of verses 1-5?

   c. How does Isaiah's description of the Messiah fit the principle found in 1 Samuel 16:7?

   d. How do Peter's words in 1 Peter 3:3-6 add to understanding God's perspective on the external versus the internal of a person's life?

e. If the Bible gives no attention to Christ's earthly appearance, is there an application to be made to the life of the Christian? How do we find the balance in a world that focuses so much on fashion and outward appearance?

2. What did Paul tell the Christians in the cities of Lystra, Iconium, and Antioch? (Acts 14:22)

   a. What had happened in Lystra that made Paul say this? (Acts 14:19-20)

   b. How do Paul's words support what Peter wrote in 1 Peter 4:12?

   c. Both Paul and Peter are referring to trials for the sake of Jesus. But how can their words apply to any kind of suffering or hardship we experience?

d. How do the words of Peter and Paul apply to John the apostle on Patmos? Why was John suffering?

e. Why does Peter say we should rejoice when we suffer for Christ? (1 Peter 4:13) How was John "partaking of Christ's sufferings" on Patmos?

f. Why did Paul say we "glory in tribulation"? (Romans 5:3-5)

g. How does Peter's phrase "when His glory is revealed" apply to John's experience on Patmos? (verse 13)

h. Why should you not be surprised when you suffer for being a Christian?

*Christ in the Midst of His Churches* • 19

i. Why should you not be surprised at other kinds of suffering in a fallen world?

j. If Christ allowed His apostles to suffer for Him, should we be surprised when we suffer as His followers? Why or why not?

---

**DID YOU KNOW?**

According to Wikipedia.com, the modern Greek island of Patmos is in the Aegean Sea closer to the coast of Turkey than to Greece. The Municipality of Patmos includes the islands of Patmos, Arkoi, Marathos, and several tiny uninhabited islands with a total population of 3,047 (in 2011). The Eastern Orthodox Church dominates the spiritual life of Patmos with many references to the apostle John's exile: the Monastery of Saint John the Theologian, the Cave of the Apocalypse, and the Patmian School, a Greek seminary. The Cave of the Apocalypse is the traditional site where John received the vision recorded in the book of Revelation.

# LESSON 2

# Losing Your First Love: The Letter to the Church in Ephesus

*Revelation 2:1-7*

*In this lesson we discover how easy it is to leave our first love and how we can return.*

---
**OUTLINE**
---

It is normal to be excited about new things and to grow passive about them over time. It can even happen in our relationship with Jesus. The excitement of meeting and following Him can become a routine. When that happens, we must remember, repent, and repeat our original passion.

I. The Destination of the Letter

II. The Description of Christ

III. The Diagnosis of the Church
   A. It Was a Dynamic Church
   B. It Was a Dedicated Church
   C. It Was a Determined Church
   D. It Was a Disciplined Church
   E. It Was a Discerning Church
   F. It Was a Declining Church

IV. The Demand of the Church
   A. Remember
   B. Repent
   C. Repeat

## OVERVIEW

In 2011 I released a book titled *I Never Thought I'd See the Day!—Culture at the Crossroads*. The book was about the slow drift away from biblical principles that is happening in our culture. Between the time I turned the manuscript in to the publisher and the time the book was released, I could have added even more chapters! Things were happening so quickly in our culture—and still are today—that I could have written a new chapter every month, maybe even every week. Today, five years later, there is no slowdown. If my hope were not in the Lord, it would be easy to become discouraged over the state of our nation. Sadly, the moral and spiritual drift is not just in our society but in our churches as well.

If the culture is drifting in the wrong direction (as well as some churches), we have to ask ourselves, What about me? Am I drifting away from biblical principles without even knowing it? After all, what are cultures and churches if not collections of individuals?

Jesus Christ commissioned the apostle John to write down His admonitions to seven churches in John's day about their spiritual condition. Revelation 2-3 contains the text of those seven letters. Because the book of Revelation would ultimately make its way to all the churches, and the book contains all seven letters, all the churches then and all the churches now can read Christ's seven letters and benefit from them. We may not live in Asia Minor in the first century, but the seven letters to the seven churches are meant for us nonetheless.

As we study all seven letters in this study guide, there are three perspectives to bear in mind:

1. Primary association. These were historical churches in seven cities: Ephesus, Smyrna, Pergamum, Thyatira, Sardis, Philadelphia, and Laodicea. We have to read the letters first in their historical contexts and then make application to our own lives.

2. Personal application. Like all Scripture, these letters are profitable for Christians of all eras (2 Timothy 3:16). Because there is "nothing new under the sun" (Ecclesiastes 1:9), the problems noted in the seven churches will bring to mind churches you have been a part of. The goal is not to criticize but to correct, beginning with ourselves. No one's opinion about the Church is more important than that of the Head of the Church, Jesus Christ (Ephesians 5:23;

Colossians 1:18). So whatever Jesus says to the Christians in those seven churches, we need to apply to ourselves and our churches.

3. Prophetic anticipation. Many scholars agree that the seven churches bear a striking resemblance to seven ages of church history since the letters were written. The first letter to the church at Ephesus represents the apostolic church and the last letter to the church at Laodicea describes the church on earth at the end of the age when Christ returns.

So the seven letters have primary, personal, and prophetic perspectives. We begin our study with the letter to the church in Ephesus.

## THE DESTINATION OF THE LETTER (REVELATION 2:1A)

The first letter was addressed to the church in Ephesus, the most prominent church in Asia Minor (the same church to which Paul's letter of Ephesians is addressed). Ephesus was a large, cosmopolitan city centered on the worship of the goddess Diana (or Artemis). Paul spent nearly three years ministering in Ephesus, the longest he stayed in any city on his missionary journeys. Paul appointed Timothy to lead the church at Ephesus and wrote him two letters during his tenure as pastor. We believe that the apostle John became leader of the church in Ephesus following Timothy, from which he was exiled to Patmos.

## THE DESCRIPTION OF CHRIST (REVELATION 2:1B)

At the beginning of each of the seven letters, Christ introduces Himself citing some aspect of who He is. At the beginning of the letter to Ephesus He calls Himself, "He who holds the seven stars in His right hand, who walks in the midst of the seven golden lampstands."

The book of Revelation (not "revelations," plural) is the revelation of Jesus Christ. That is, a revelation of Christ Himself and a revelation "of" (given by) Him concerning the present and future. Here He reveals Himself as the One who stands in the midst of all the churches. He is the One with authority to address the churches and reveal Himself to them. Christ was in the midst of the first-century churches and the twenty-first-century churches as well.

# THE DIAGNOSIS OF THE CHURCH (REVELATION 2:2-4)

The next three verses comprise the diagnosis of the church. For the church of Ephesus, the diagnosis was mostly positive (verses 2-3). But there is one diagnosis that is negative (verse 4). First, the positive.

### It Was a Dynamic Church (verse 2)

Christ's first words to the Ephesian church were, "I know your works." John Stott summarizes their work: "Its members were fully occupied, entertaining the lonely and nursing the sick, teaching the young and visiting the aged. No doubt some gave hours of their time to making and mending, sewing and knitting for the church. Others spent their leisure hours writing and cooking and cleaning and organizing. The church of Ephesus was a veritable beehive of industry. Their toil was famous. Every member was doing something for Christ."[1]

In our focus on salvation by grace through faith (Ephesians 2:8-9), good works often are deemphasized. But they shouldn't be (Ephesians 2:10). One of the purposes of the local church is to "stir up love and good works" (Hebrews 10:24). We are not saved *by* good works but we are saved *for* good works. Because of the good works of the Ephesian Christians, "all who dwelt in Asia heard the word of the Lord Jesus, both Jews and Greeks" (Acts 19:10).

### It Was a Dedicated Church (verse 2)

Besides good works, Christ commended them for their "labor" which included spreading the Gospel. "Works" refers to activity; "labor" refers to working to the point of exhaustion. They weren't working comfortably; they were expending all their energy in serving Christ. In modern churches with paid staff, it is often forgotten that the role of pastor-teachers is "for the equipping of the saints for the work of ministry" (Ephesians 4:12). Every Christian's full-time calling is "the work of ministry." The Ephesian church had taken to heart what Paul wrote in his letter to them.

### It Was a Determined Church (verse 3)

Christ wrote that the Ephesians had "persevered and [had] patience" in their work and labor. Their patience was not passive, but active. They were patiently enduring suffering as they went about serving Christ. Biblical patience is proactive in its endurance. When Paul ministered in Ephesus, there was both spiritual and physical opposition and persecution (Acts 19). Paul established a template for the believers in how to patiently endure.

The great London preacher Charles Spurgeon describes the kind of "grit" possessed by the Ephesian Christians:

"Pray God to send a few men with what the Americans call "grit" in them; men, who, when they know a thing to be right, will not turn away, or turn aside, or stop; men, who will persevere all the more because there are difficulties to meet or foes to encounter; who stand all the more true to their Master because they are opposed; who the more they are thrust into the fire, the hotter they become; who just like the bow, the further the string is drawn, the more powerfully it sends forth its arrows, and so the more they are trodden upon, the more mighty will they become in the cause of truth against error."[2]

## *It Was a Disciplined Church (verse 2)*

Christ identified the discipline of the Ephesians when He said, "I know . . . that you cannot bear those who are evil." They would not tolerate evil or unrighteousness in their midst; they exercised church discipline when it was needed (see 1 Corinthians 5:1-13).

## *It Was a Discerning Church (verse 2)*

The Ephesians' discernment was evident when they "tested" those who claimed to be apostles "and have found them to be liars." There was no shortage of false apostles in the early years of the church—men who claimed to have been granted authority by Christ's true apostles to lead churches (see 2 Corinthians 11:1-15). But the Ephesian church rejected these false apostles; they had the discernment needed to separate truth from error.

Paul had actually warned the elders in Ephesus about the coming of "savage wolves [who] will come in among you, not sparing the flock" (Acts 20:29). It apparently had happened, but the Ephesian church allowed them no access to the flock. Discernment is based on doctrine. Pastors and church leaders must be able to separate truth from error.

## *It Was a Declining Church (verse 4)*

Christ commended the Ephesian church in five ways before turning to His one correction: "Nevertheless I have this against you, that you have left your first love." Everything about the Ephesian church looked good on the outside, but inwardly they had heart trouble. Their devotion to Christ was waning. It is a dramatic reminder that it is possible to do the works of ministry without being in love with Jesus Christ—as if the Church is nothing but a corporate structure.

"First love" is that fervent, excited love that every new Christian feels when meeting Christ. It's like the love of a couple on their honeymoon when they have eyes only for one another. It's the unashamed, unabashed love of those who are not afraid to identify with Jesus in every dimension of their lives. The Weymouth translation of the New Testament puts verse 4 this way: "Yet I have this against you, that you no longer love Me as you did at first."

It's a bad thing to know that Christ has something "against us" as He had against the Ephesians. When that is true, it is time for us to make things right. Without a pure love for the Savior, eventually our good works will lack the power and persuasion they are meant to have. When a relationship with Jesus turns to a religion, we have left our first love.

Thirty years prior to these words from Christ, Paul had concluded his letter to the Ephesians this way: "Grace be with all those who love our Lord Jesus Christ in sincerity. Amen" (Ephesians 6:24). So in a few decades, the same church had allowed their love to grow cold. They had drifted away from their first love. Today's Church exists in a world drifting ever further from biblical standards. We must make sure that our present love for Christ is the same as our first love.

# THE DEMAND OF THE CHURCH (REVELATION 2:5)

Such a letter would be disheartening if it ended there. Fortunately, it does not; Christ gives the Ephesian church instructions on how to return to their first love—a three-part formula.

## *Remember*

Christ's first admonition is to "Remember therefore from where you have fallen." If we have left something or someone, the first step is to remember where we started. In this case, it means remembering, thinking back on, what one's relationship with Christ was when we were first saved and growing in Him. That's not difficult to do. We can all remember the first years of our walk with the Lord, the discovery of what life could really be like. New Christians are excited about church, reading the Bible, fellowshipping with other believers, inviting someone to church or a Bible study—it's a whole new world! You lived your life as a matter of trust: God said it, you believed it, and that settled it.

But somehow, almost imperceptibly, that enthusiasm and energy can dissipate. We become "professional Christians" who go through the motions (doing "the works") without the passion. Our Christian life becomes a matter of routine instead of a relationship with the living Christ who saved us and delivered us into eternal life.

The Greek verb form used in "remember" in verse 5 is present active imperative. The imperative mood adds a command dimension. Remembering is not, in other words, a suggestion. And the present active form suggests "keep on remembering." So Christ is saying, "You must always keep on remembering your starting place in the Christian life—Me."

One of my favorite choruses that my church sings on Sunday mornings is called "We Will Remember." One of the lines says, "I still remember the day He saved me . . . and I will never be the same." That's what Christ was telling the Ephesians and what He is telling us.

## *Repent*

The next logical step after remembering where we started and realizing where we are now is to repent: "Remember therefore from where you have fallen; repent . . . ." Repentance means to change your mind; it means to reverse course and go in the opposite direction. It is less a matter of weeping and wailing than it is a conscious choice of the will, a decision to (first) turn and (then) return.

John Stott has written, "Repentance is resolutely and completely to turn one's back on all known sin. Jesus Christ does not advocate conjuring up of emotional experience. He does not urge the Ephesian Christians to feel bad about sins. It is not what they feel about them which matters, so much as what they do about them."[3]

If you have drifted away from the Lord, you probably know it and you probably feel bad about it. But that is not repentance. Only when you turn around and go back to where you began with Christ will you do what He told the Ephesians to do. Remember: You never get back on the right road by remaining on the wrong road. Turn around and go back to the crossroads. Get off the wrong road and start walking on the right road. In other words, repent.

## *Repeat*

After remembering and repenting and getting back to the place where you began, there is a third step: Repeat the former good works. Christ praised the Ephesians for their works, their labor, their patience, their discipline, and their discernment. What they needed to do was "the first works" all over again. For us, that means returning to what we did when we first became a Christian—the spiritual disciplines that kept us close to Christ and motivated to follow Him.

In 1 Corinthians 13 the apostle Paul characterizes biblical love with a series of action words. That is, love is a verb as well as a noun. The same is true about our love for Christ—it is demonstrated by actions that show our love for Him. Those are the actions to which we need to return. The way we return to our first love is to go back to the fundamentals of the Christian life that we learned and practiced as a new follower of Jesus. You can create your own list of things that excited you as a new believer and compare it with your spiritual life today. Where there are differences you'll find directions on how to return to your first love.

Christ continued with the Ephesian church: If you do not "repent and do the first works, I will come to you quickly and remove your lampstand from its place." That is, the church's influence and power would be removed. There is a price to pay for drifting away from the Lord. Today, Ephesus is no longer a light for Christ.

I recall reading a statement by someone that captures the heart of Christ's letter to the Ephesians: "On my way to the Savior I ran into serving. I started serving and never got to the Savior." There is nothing wrong with service, of course. But if it, or any other "good works" ever replaces our love and passion for Jesus Christ Himself, we will find we have left our first love.

Where are you today? Ask God to use Christ's letter to the Ephesians to help you remember the place where it all began. And to make your way back there.

Notes:

1. John Stott, *What Christ Thinks of the Church* (Grand Rapids, MI: Wm. B. Eerdmans Publishing Company, 1958), 23.
2. Charles Spurgeon, from a sermon entitled "The Jeer of Sarcasm, and the Retort of Piety," delivered April 8, 1860.
3. John Stott, *What Christ Thinks of the Church* (Grand Rapids, MI: Wm. B. Eerdmans Publishing Company, 1958), 32.

## APPLICATION

1. What does 2 Timothy 3:16 suggest about the value of Christ's words to the seven churches for the Church today?

   a. In spite of nearly 1,900 years difference, why do the words of Ecclesiastes 1:9 apply to finding modern solutions to ancient church problems?

   b. According to this lesson, which of the seven churches might today's Church look to for the most relevant application?

2. From this lesson, note the three perspectives that must be included in the study of the letters to the seven churches and why each perspective is important.

   a. _____ association:

   b. _____ application:

   c. _____ anticipation:

*Losing Your First Love: The Letter to the Church in Ephesus* • 29

3. From Acts 19-20, answer the following questions:

   a. How did Paul correct the understanding of some disciples of John the Baptist? (19:1-7)

   b. Where did Paul go first to preach in Ephesus? (19:8)

   c. What time references are found that indicate how long he stayed in Ephesus? (19:8, 10; 20:31)

   d. What kind of signs mentioned by Paul in 2 Corinthians 12:12 did Paul accomplish in Ephesus? (19:11-12)

e. What spiritual opposition did Paul encounter in Ephesus? What was the result? (19:13-17)

f. Why was Paul attacked by some in Ephesus? (19:23-28)

g. What connection do you find between Paul's warning to the Ephesian elders in 20:28-31 and Christ's commendation in Revelation 2:2b?

h. When Paul made his final good-byes to the Ephesian elders, what do verses 20:36-38 reveal about their relationship?

4. Based on notes from this lesson, what was the evidence of the Ephesian church's . . .

   a. Dynamism (Revelation 2:2)

   b. Dedication (Revelation 2:2)

   c. Determination (Revelation 2:3)

   d. Discipline (Revelation 2:2)

   e. Discernment (Revelation 2:2)

5. What was the one thing Christ had to say against the Ephesian church? (Revelation 2:4)

   a. How would you interpret that in practical terms?

   b. What three steps did Christ outline (mentioned in the lesson) as a remedy? (Revelation 2:5)

      1. _____

      2. _____

      3. _____

6. How would you contrast the passion of your Christian life today with your passion as a new believer in Christ?

## DID YOU KNOW?

The book of Revelation takes its name from the book's first verse: "The Revelation of Jesus Christ, which God gave Him to show His servants." In Greek, the word "revelation" comes from the verb *apokalupto* which is made of two words: *apo* (from, away from) and *kalupto* (to cover). So *apokalupto* means to take a cover from or to uncover. Therefore, a revelation is an uncovering or a revealing. Besides the uncovering of the details of the future, there is another uncovering in the book of Revelation: the revealing of Jesus Christ Himself who has been "concealed" in heaven since His ascension from earth. Both Christ and the future are revealed in the book of Revelation.

# LESSON 3

# THE SUFFERING CHURCH: THE LETTER TO THE CHURCH IN SMYRNA

*Revelation 2:8-11*

*In this lesson we discover how it is possible to endure persecution for the sake of Christ.*

## OUTLINE

Christians in developed countries today think little about being persecuted for their faith. But there are churches in the world where such persecution is a daily reality. Such was the ancient church in Smyrna. Christ's words to that church can prepare all believers for what might come.

I. **The Church**

II. **Why the Church in Smyrna Suffered**
   A. Pressure
   B. Poverty
   C. Persecution

III. **Our Lord's Counsel to the Church**
   A. Be Fearless
   B. Be Faithful

IV. **Conclusion**
   A. The Reputation of Christ Was Better Than the Reputation of Rome
   B. The Recognition of Christ Was Better Than the Recognition of Rome
   C. The Riches of Christ Were Better Than the Riches of Rome
   D. The Reckoning of Time by Christ Was Better Than the Reckoning of Time by Rome
   E. The Rewards of Christ Were Better Than the Rewards of Rome

## OVERVIEW

The Old Testament book of Job contains the longest example of people trying to help a friend who was suffering. Unfortunately, it's not a great example. Job's three friends did little to comfort Job. They started off right—they just sat with Job and empathized with him in silence for a week. But as soon as they started talking, it all went downhill. They said Job's suffering was because he had somehow offended God. So their strategy was not particularly helpful.

But there are better examples—not as long, but definitely better. In the New Testament much is written to believers in Christ who were suffering for Christ, suffering through no fault of their own except for being faithful. What would you say to such people? It's not a theoretical question. People all around the world today are suffering for their faithfulness to Christ. And the day could come in the future when we suffer for the same reason.

The second of the seven letters to first-century churches contains Christ's words to a church suffering for its faith—the church in Smyrna.

Smyrna (modern Izmir) was 35 miles north of ancient Ephesus (modern Selçuk) in Asia Minor (modern Turkey). Founded as a Greek colony around 1000 B.C., it was destroyed in 600 B.C., then rebuilt by one of Alexander the Great's generals around 300 B.C. It was a matter of pride with the inhabitants of Smyrna that their city had died and had lived again.

Historians consider Smyrna to have been the most beautiful city the Greeks ever built. A prominent hill was called "the crown of Smyrna" (remember that word "crown"). There was a huge amphitheater that sat 20,000 people. Smyrna was called "The First City of Asia" and "The Glory of Asia." During the Roman period, the worship of Caesar for the eastern part of the empire was centered in Smyrna. Smyrna's name is derived from an aromatic resin, its chief export (see "Did You Know?").

## THE CHURCH

The church in Smyrna was likely started as an outreach from the church in Ephesus. Paul was in Ephesus for three years (Acts 20:31), during which time "all who dwelt in Asia heard the word of the Lord Jesus" (Acts 19:10). This is one of two of the seven churches to which Christ said nothing negative. Like the aromatic oil (smyrna) released by the crushing of a local plant, the believers in Smyrna were releasing the fragrant aroma of Christ in spite of their suffering.

# Why the Church in Smyrna Suffered (Revelation 2:9)

The believers in Smyrna suffered because they did not worship the popular pagan gods or the Roman emperors. Smyrna was the first city to build a temple to honor Rome and the worship of its deified emperors. Citizens of the Roman Empire were loyal to Rome because of all the benefits Rome brought to them: peace, roads, defense from enemies, prosperity, laws, and more. When Rome's emperors began proclaiming themselves as deity, it was a small step for Roman citizens to go along. To love Rome was to love its emperors—and worship them.

The apostle John was an example of a Christian leader in Asia Minor who would not worship Caesar and was thus exiled. Christians were considered disloyal to Rome. Rome allowed different religions to exist as long as the people would worship the emperor above all others. The Christians refused to do that and were tortured terribly for their faith: burning, boiling, crucifixion, and death by wild animals were only some of the ways their faith was tested.

The suffering of the Smyrna church can be summarized from Christ's letter to them with three words: pressure, poverty, and persecution.

## *Pressure*

Christ wrote to the Smyrna church, "I know your . . . tribulation." The Greek word for "tribulation" literally means pressure—like placing a boulder on a person's chest until it crushes him to death. Or like the weight of a millstone crushing grain into flour or grapes into juice. It is a grizzly image when applied to humanity. But it's what the Christians in Smyrna were experiencing—constant pressure.

## *Poverty*

The second thing Christ said He knew about them was their "poverty." The Greek word behind "poverty" meant absolute destitution (there were other less dramatic words). It referred to a person who had nothing—penniless and poor. Their poverty was due to their Christian faith. They were banned in the city from earning a living and were robbed of what they had. There was no romantic heroism associated with this persecution. It likely meant starving to death for one's faith.

## *Persecution*

Not only was their persecution from Romans and religious pagans, there was persecution from so-called Jews. Christ wrote, "And I know the blasphemy of those who say they are Jews and are not, but are a synagogue of Satan." These so-called Jews were Jews in name only who attacked the Christian believers for their worship of Jesus (Romans 2:28-29). Instead of being part of a true Jewish synagogue, Christ says they represented "a synagogue of Satan." Not only were there false apostles in Asia Minor, there were false Jews as well.

It is important to remember that today, in different parts of the world, there are religious people who think nothing of attacking and persecuting Christians. Some Christians today suffer the same kind of persecution as the believers in Smyrna.

# OUR LORD'S COUNSEL TO THE CHURCH (REVELATION 2:10)

Christ responds to the church's situation with something *not to do* and something *to do*. These two admonitions will serve today's suffering Christians well.

### *Be Fearless*

First, something not to do: "Do not fear any of those things which you are about to suffer." In fairness to the Smyrna Christians, is saying, "Do not fear" actually helpful? It reminds us of David's words in Psalm 23:4—even when facing death, "I will fear no evil." It is one thing for David to say "I will fear no evil" because he had actually been in the valley of the shadow of death. Not fearing evil was his choice. But does it help to tell others, "Do not fear"?

Yes, if that person is a Christian. Why? Because Christ is Lord over all of life's circumstances. Paul wrote that there is nothing that can separate us from the love of God in Christ Jesus (Romans 8:35-39). We must choose to believe that or not. We are not required to be fearful in scary situations. Yes, it is a natural human response. But we live *supernatural* lives through the power of Christ in us. We can live fearless lives.

### *Be Faithful*

Next, we are to be "faithful until death." Instead of being fearful, Christ says, be faithful. Given the intensity of the persecution in Smyrna, I believe Christ was saying, "Yes, you may lose your life for My sake, but be faithful until the end." John Stott explains:

"We need to remember that faith and faithfulness are the same word in the Greek language. This is understandable because it is from faith that we get faithfulness. Trust in Christ and show ourselves to be trustworthy. Rely on Christ and we shall be reliable. Depend on Christ and we shall be dependable. Have faith in Christ and we shall be faithful—faithful, if necessary, even unto death. The way to lose fear is to gain faith."[1]

# Conclusion

Though this is a short letter, there are many lessons for the Church in every age. They can be grouped under this principle: the opposite of fear is faith—faith in God, faith in what God has said, faith in who God is, and faith in what He has promised us.

### *The Reputation of Christ Was Better Than the Reputation of Rome (Revelation 2:8)*

Christ stands above any worldly source of power or authority: "These things says the First and the Last, who was dead, and came to life." "The First and the Last" is the phrase Christ used to dispel fear in the apostle John in their first encounter (Revelation 1:7). And it can dispel fear in all who believe that Christ is the First and the Last.

This phrase is a claim to eternity. For people facing persecution and the potential of death, what could be more reassuring than the promise of eternal protection? Only Christ has defeated death and the grave by the Resurrection. Only Christ was there at the beginning of time and will be there at the end of time. Christ's own persecution led to death, yet He still lives—and the same will be true for any who die in Him.

Smyrna was an ancient city that had died and come back to life. It was the greatest city in the eastern part of the Empire. It was the first city and the last word in beauty. But the believers in Smyrna were citizens of an even greater kingdom whose King is the eternal God. And that is where faith conquers fear. If we truly believe that Christ gained victory over death, we will not fear death or any other hardship.

### *The Recognition of Christ Was Better Than the Recognition of Rome (Revelation 2:9)*

If Christ knows what we are going through, it doesn't matter if anybody else does. He said, "I know your works, tribulation, and poverty." Most modern translations of the Bible omit the word "works" from this verse. (It's a matter of Greek manuscript evidence.) That means Christ said, "I know your tribulation and poverty." The most important thing to note is that Christ's knowledge is not purely intellectual. This word for "know" means to know by experience. Christ was not only *sympathetic* toward the Smyrna church but, more importantly, *empathetic*. He had been where they were.

Christ came to earth having given up the riches of heaven. For three years He had "nowhere to lay His head" (Matthew 8:20). For three years He endured the daily pressure of lies, slander, false accusations, and ultimately being brutally whipped and murdered. There was nothing that the believers in Smyrna experienced—not persecution or poverty—that He had not experienced.

Hebrews 4:15 says, "For we do not have a High Priest who cannot sympathize with our weaknesses, but was in all points tempted as we are, yet without sin." There is nothing we will be faced with in life that Christ has not already faced and conquered.

One writer has said, "He took cognizance of every sorrow; His heart felt every pang; he counted every tear. The weight of oppression was fully known to him, and the wealth of His divine sympathy went out to his people . . . and still today, not a trial passes unnoticed, nor a difficulty unobserved. Our great shepherd knows every bruise sustained by His sheep, and every suffering experienced by them, and because He too has passed through suffering, He sympathizes with his own."[2]

## *The Riches of Christ Were Better Than the Riches of Rome (Revelation 2:9)*

Smyrna was a wealthy city, and Rome was even wealthier. Yet Christ pointed out to the believers in Smyrna that, in spite of their poverty and persecution, "You are rich." What did He mean by that? He obviously meant it in a spiritual sense in the same way as His words in Matthew 6:20 about "[laying] up for yourselves treasures in heaven."

Christians are not citizens of earth but citizens of heaven. They do not depend on earthly riches for their sustenance but on the riches of heaven. Paul wrote that, even though we may be poor, we can make many rich, "having nothing and yet possessing all things" (2 Corinthians 6:10). This is yet another kingdom paradox —being poor in one sense yet rich in another sense. Second Corinthians 8:9 says that through Christ's poverty we have become rich. In Christ we have riches and wealth of which the world knows nothing.

Christians do not count wealth as the world counts it. There are poverty-stricken churches all over the world who, while poor in terms of material things, are rich in the kingdom treasures of love, hope, patience, and faithfulness to Christ. There is no guarantee that earthly riches are a source of contentment and joy. The fear of losing those riches can become an all-consuming preoccupation (see the parable in Luke 12:16-20). Some of the most precious people I've ever known in my life have very little in a material sense. But they have joy and peace in their life knowing that they are a child of God and are loved by Him. If you asked them, they would say, "I am truly rich with wealth I can never lose."

## *The Reckoning of Time by Christ Was Better Than the Reckoning of Time by Rome (Revelation 2:10)*

In Revelation 2:10 we find these words of Christ: "Do not fear any of those things which you are about to suffer. Indeed, the devil is about to throw some of you into prison, that you may be tested, and you will have tribulation ten days." What did He mean by "ten days"? There has been no end to the speculation about this time reference in the letter to Smyrna.

Some think it refers to 10 years of coming persecution for the church in Smyrna. Others suggest it refers to Roman persecution that came in the second and third centuries. Historians tell us there were 10 waves of persecution that took place under 10 Roman emperors ending with the reign of Diocletian.

While it could mean any of those, I believe "ten days" is a simple reference to the brevity of what the Smyrna Christians were enduring compared to eternity. Their suffering would be brief; eternity will be never-ending. Jesus is saying to them, "This is going to seem like a long time; but in comparison to eternity, it's just 10 days." This is certainly consistent with Paul's words in 2 Corinthians 4:17: "For our light affliction, which is but for a moment, is working for us a far more exceeding and eternal weight of glory."

The point is this: Time is in God's hands. Even when troubles seem to go on forever in our life, God remains in control. His plans in our life are defined by His purposes. When God puts a number on the days the Smyrna church would suffer, He is saying, "There is a limit. This will not go on forever." When we know that God has a purpose, it gives us hope and endurance in the midst of our trial. We must remember this lesson from Smyrna when we are in trials of our own.

## *The Rewards of Christ Were Better Than the Rewards of Rome (Revelation 2:10-11)*

Everyone in Smyrna knew about the prominent hill known as "the crown of Smyrna." But Christ promised the believers in that church an even better crown: "Be faithful until death, and I will give you the crown of life."

This is the same crown described by the apostle James: "Blessed is the man who endures temptation; for when he has been approved, he will receive the crown of life which the Lord has promised to those who love Him" (James 1:12). Those crowns will ultimately be offered to Christ Himself in acts of worship at the Judgment Seat of Christ (Revelation 4:10).

The crown of life is not the only reward promised by Christ: "He who overcomes shall not be hurt by the second death." There are two deaths in Scripture. The first we all experience, the death at the end of our earthly life. The second death is for those who are judged when Christ returns and are consigned to an eternity apart from God. Believers in Christ will be spared that judgment and "will not be hurt by the second death" (Revelation 20:5-6). Everyone in the world knows about the first death, and many live in fear of it. But it is the second death that is more critical. We can do nothing about the first death; the second death we can avoid if we so choose by placing our faith in Christ.

The Christian church in Smyrna had nothing to fear from martyrdom. No matter how cruel the torture, the Romans could never separate them from God. Every believer in Christ today should take comfort in that same truth: Nothing can separate us from the love of God in Christ Jesus.

Notes:

1. John Stott, *What Christ Thinks of the Church* (Grand Rapids, MI: Wm. B. Eerdmans Publishing Company, 1958), 46.
2. Fred A. Tatford, *Prophecy's Last Word—An Exposition of Revelation* (Grand Rapids, Zondervan, 1967), 45.

## APPLICATION

1. Why is it possible that the church in Smyrna (as well as others) was planted by the church in Ephesus? (Acts 19:10; 20:31)

2. How did the apostle Paul define who was a genuine Jew and who wasn't? (Romans 2:28-29)

   a. Could the same distinction be made about true Christians? In what way?

   b. For a Christian, what might be the equivalent of being born a Jew and undergoing circumcision as external signs of religion? Why are external signs not what really matters?

3. If you encouraged a fellow Christian by saying, "Don't be afraid," and they responded, "That's easy for you to say!" what would you tell them?

   a. Why did David say he would "fear no evil" in Psalm 23:4-6?

   b. Why is faith the opposite of fear? Why is fear always based on an unknown future?

   c. How can walking by sight (or the inability to "see" the future) lead to fear? (2 Corinthians 5:7)

4. Read Romans 8:35-39.

   a. List all the things Paul says cannot separate us from God's love in Christ. (verses 35, 38-39)

   b. How does "nor anything else in all creation" (verse 39, NIV) cover any circumstance in your life that could lead to fear?

   c. How does the phrase "more than conquerors" in verse 37 parallel what Christ is saying to the church in Smyrna? Why should they have been confident in spite of their circumstances?

5. Briefly review 1 Corinthians 15 to determine Paul's theme in that chapter. How does that theme apply to those who are possibly facing death for their faith? (see verses 51-54)

a. What is the difference between the first and second deaths, as mentioned in Scripture and discussed in this lesson?

b. Why does the believer in Christ have no fear of the second death?

6. What would you fear most about being persecuted for your faith in Christ? What have you learned in this lesson that would encourage you in such a situation?

---

### DID YOU KNOW?

Smyrna (Greek *Smurna*) was named for its principle export, an aromatic resin known as myrrh (*smurna*). "Myrrh" is mentioned three times in the New Testament. Myrrh was one of three gifts presented by the magi to the baby Jesus (Matthew 2:11). Myrrh was mixed with wine and offered to Jesus at His crucifixion to dull His pain (Mark 15:23). And when Jesus was buried, His body was wrapped in cloths with myrrh and aloe folded in (John 19:39). When Isaiah foretold the second coming of the Messiah, he mentioned gold and incense but not myrrh (Isaiah 60:6). Myrrh was a symbol of suffering, appropriate for His first coming. But when He comes again, myrrh will not be needed.

LESSON 4

# THE CHURCH OF SATAN'S CITY: THE LETTER TO THE CHURCH IN PERGAMOS

*Revelation 2:12-17*

*In this lesson we discover how corruption and compromise can weaken God's Church.*

## OUTLINE

One of society's central themes today is toleration—especially directed at Christians. We are expected to tolerate everyone and everything. But toleration has been the downfall of many churches throughout history. The danger is seen clearly in the ancient church in Pergamos.

I. The Destination of the Letter: Pergamos

II. The Designation of the Lord

III. The Diagnosis of the Church
   A. He Knew the Circumstances of Their Faith
   B. He Knew the Conviction of Their Faith
   C. He Knew the Courage of Their Faith
   D. He Knew the Compromise of Their Faith

IV. The Demand of the Church

V. The Problems of Pergamos Lived Out in History

## OVERVIEW

Does the town or city where you live have a nickname or label? Many cities do. I live near San Diego which we love to call "America's Greatest City." Los Angeles is known as "The City of Angels." New York City is "The Big Apple" or "The City that Never Sleeps." Detroit is "The Motor City," Chicago is "The Windy City," and Las Vegas is "Sin City."

In this lesson we're going to read Christ's words to the church in a city that He Himself named—and it's not a pretty name: Satan's City.

# THE DESTINATION OF THE LETTER: PERGAMOS

When Revelation was written, Pergamos was the capital of Rome's government in Asia. Built on top of a large hill, residents of Pergamos could see the Mediterranean Sea some 15 miles to the west. Renowned biblical scholar Edwin Yamauchi provides some helpful background on Pergamos.

"The city was a cultural center, famous for its library. The library, located on top of the acropolis, was second only to the library in Alexandria. The large hall which served as a reading room measured 44 feet by 52 feet. The library in Pergamos is said to have held two hundred thousand volumes when Mark Antony offered it to Cleopatra. When Egypt refused to sell papyrus to the Pergamenes, they treated sheep and goatskins to produce "parchment." (The Latin of "parchment" is "pergamentum.") Even today, when you are graduated from college, your diploma is called a "sheepskin."[1]

# THE DESIGNATION OF THE LORD (REVELATION 2:12)

As in each of the seven letters, Christ introduces Himself to the church at Pergamos, this time calling Himself "He who has the sharp two-edged sword." The sword was obviously a symbol of power and judgment. The fact that it proceeds from Christ's mouth is an indication that His words bear the same power to judge as a sword would to destroy one's enemies. It is another indication that Christ is the true authority, not the Roman officials in Pergamos.

# The Diagnosis of the Church (Revelation 2:13-15)

Christ's words point out why Pergamos could have been called "Satan's City": "I know . . . where you dwell, where Satan's throne is. And you hold fast to My name, and did not deny My faith even in the days in which Antipas was My faithful martyr, who was killed among you, where Satan dwells" (verse 13).

There are four things Christ knew about the faith of the church in Pergamos.

### *He Knew the Circumstances of Their Faith (Revelation 2:13)*

Pergamos was a center of paganism and idolatry. Of no other city did Christ make the devastating connection He made to Pergamos—the seat of Satan's throne. Some scholars think the allusion to a "throne" may have been based on the amazing altar of Zeus in Pergamos. Built on the Acropolis, it was the most famous and ornate altar in the world—100 feet square, 40 feet high, with impressive sculptures surrounding its base. Parts of that altar now reside in a museum in Berlin. It could have been the reason for Christ's allusion to "Satan's throne."

Pergamos was the center of the worship of Asclepius, the god of healing. Temples to Asclepius were the nearest thing the ancient world had to modern hospitals. People from all over Asia journeyed to Pergamos in search of healing at one of the temples devoted to Asclepius. So the Christians in Pergamos were surrounded by pagan beliefs and practices.

### *He Knew the Conviction of Their Faith (Revelation 2:13)*

In spite of the pagan pressure upon them, Christ commended the Pergamos church: "And you hold fast to My name." Very simply, these words show that no matter our circumstances it is possible to hold fast to our faith in Christ. There could be pressure and persecution of all sorts but that doesn't mean we can't be faithful. We can! In fact, I wonder sometimes if it's not easier to be faithful in situations where our faith is challenged every day. Where we live, our faith is rarely, if ever, challenged; and it is easy to become complacent. In Pergamos, when a Christian confessed his faith, he did it knowing the consequences.

## *He Knew the Courage of Their Faith (Revelation 2:13)*

Christ also recognized their courage: "And [you] did not deny My faith even in the days in which Antipas was My faithful martyr, who was killed among you, where Satan dwells."

This Antipas is mentioned nowhere else in Scripture, and we know nothing of him from history. But no one escapes Jesus' attention! The Lord who is the First and the Last sees all who are faithful to Him. And Antipas was one of those; his name actually means "against all." He stood against all opposing forces and would not recant his faith in Christ, and it cost him his life.

Just as Christ knew of Antipas' faithfulness unto death, He knows of your faithfulness to Him as well. Even when no one else sees or knows the times when you hold fast to your faith, Jesus does.

## *He Knew the Compromise of Their Faith (Revelation 2:14-15)*

In spite of their faithfulness in some areas, the Christians in Pergamos had compromised their faith in others. Christ says nothing negative about the churches in Smyrna and Philadelphia. But all the rest had failed in some way. The Pergamos church had allowed idolatry to creep into their congregation. Remember: they lived in the midst of Satanic influence. Some of the devil's ministers had made their way into the church to promote the "doctrine of Balaam" (verse 14).

1. The Doctrine of Balaam

Balaam was a pagan prophet in the Old Testament; he claimed the ability to influence the "gods" against one's enemies. That is, he would work "favors" for a price, irrespective of which god needed influencing.

Balak, the king of Moab, enlisted Balaam to curse Israel as she made her way through Moab on the way to the Promised Land. But the God of Israel overpowered Balaam and the prophet was unable to curse Israel. In the end, Balaam ended up blessing Israel instead of cursing Israel, much to the consternation of Balak. In return for an even larger fee, Balaam gave Balak a better idea: Get the Moabite women to seduce the Israelite men, marry them, then corrupt their religion by intermingling the worship of God with Moab's idolatry. It was successful—and God sent a plague among the Israelites as punishment, killing 24,000 Israelites (Numbers 25:1 ff.). In short, the doctrine of Balaam was this: If you can't curse them, corrupt them.

That is what was happening in Pergamos. The church was tolerating evil in its midst. The apostle Peter wrote of the same problem among a different group: "They have forsaken the right way and gone astray, following the way of Balaam the son of Beor, who loved the wages of unrighteousness" (2 Peter 2:15; see also Jude 11).

The later preacher and commentator Donald Grey Barnhouse captured the essence of the doctrine of Balaam at Pergamos: "The very word 'Pergamos' has in it the same root from which we get our English word for 'bigamy' and 'polygamy.' It is the word for marriage. Pergamos signifies a mixed marriage in the most objectionable sense of the word, for it is the marriage of the organization of the Church of Jesus Christ with the world."[2]

2. The Doctrine of the Nicolaitans

But that wasn't all of which the Pergamos church was guilty. They had also allowed into the midst "those who hold the doctrine of the Nicolaitans" (verse 15). "Nicolaitans" is derived from two words that mean "to conquer the laity"—the subjugation of one group of people by another. Commentators suggest that there was an authoritarian hierarchy in the church that had gathered power unto itself, forcing the laity into a subservient status. They had forgotten Jesus' words, "For One is your Teacher, the Christ, and you are all brethren" (Matthew 23:8).

# The Demand of the Church (Revelation 2:16)

Christ did not mince words with the church at Pergamos: "Repent, or else I will come to you quickly and will fight against them with the sword of My mouth." "Them," of course, refers to those promoting the doctrines of Balaam and the Nicolaitans. The "sword of My mouth" we have seen several times already, referring to Christ's words of judgment that would destroy those who were destroying His Church.

# The Problems of Pergamos Lived Out in History

Just as Israelite men married Moabite women and corrupted the life of Israel (until judgment destroyed those who had sinned), so the church at Pergamos had married the world and its doctrines.

Has this happened in Church history? Recall from Lesson 1 in this series: The seven churches broadly represent eras of Church history. Ephesus represented the apostolic Church and Smyrna the persecuted Church during the ensuing centuries in the Roman Empire. Those two churches represent the period of apostolic expansion of the Church and then the suffering of the Church that caused the Gospel to be spread even further.

What does the church at Pergamos represent? A bit of background: For 250 years the Church suffered under the Roman emperors, most notably under Emperor Diocletian. But then Constantine became emperor and a Christian and brought the doctrine of Balaam into the Church in Rome. What Diocletian couldn't accomplish by crushing the Church, Constantine did by corrupting it.

Following the death of Diocletian early in the fourth century A.D., two Roman leaders contended to become the next emperor: Constantine in the west and Maxentius in the east. On the night before a major battle, Constantine reportedly saw a vision of the cross in the sky bearing this Latin inscription: "in hoc signo vinces" which meant, "in this sign you will conquer." Constantine won the Battle of the Milvian Bridge, declared himself a Christian, and made Christianity the official religion of the Roman Empire. He forced entire regiments of Roman soldiers to be baptized as Christians—it was either be baptized or be killed. The Church and State were officially joined with Constantine the head of both. Unfortunately, when bishops from all over the Mediterranean world later met in a conference, they carried Constantine in on a golden throne from which he presided as head of the Church. But there was never any evidence that Constantine was truly born again as a believer in Christ. Christianity was, for him, simply a unifying force in his empire. Constantine took the ancient title Pontifex Maximus and became the first pope of the "holy" Roman church. The age represented by the church at Pergamos had begun—the corruption of the Church by compromise with the world.

Pagan temples became Christian churches and heathen festivals became Christian celebrations, some of which are now celebrated on the modern Church's calendar. The late scholar and preacher W. A. Criswell describes what happened:

"The priests of Jupiter, of Juno, of Dionysius, of Bacchus, of Venus, and of Adonis, all had been paid out of the purse of Caesar. But now that Caesar was a Christian, the priests of the temples hastened to their baptism to remain on the imperial payrolls. They turned their heathen temples into churches, and they said, "These are no longer images of Jupiter or Juno or Venus; these are images of the saints." The same rituals by which they had worshipped Astarte, Aphrodite, or Venus, they now employed to worship the true Queen of Heaven. They bowed down in the same way, in the same ceremony, in the same temples, before the same idols; now the idols were named after so called Christian saints. Even the days by which the priest honored their gods were made days on the calendar to honor these saints. The astonishing thing took place overnight. Heretofore, humble homes and catacombs and dungeons had echoed with the hymns of God's children, whose singing was sometimes changed into the shouts of the martyrs as they were dragged into the arena. All of that now was past. The rags of persecution were changed for the plush silk of the imperial palace. The Pergamean period of the church had begun."[3]

The Church had married the world. And for many years to come, Rome ruled the world using the Christian Church as a tool. Walter Scott summarizes it well: "Constantine offered his gold and patronage to the church, and it eagerly swallowed the bait, sacrificed its conscience and allegiance to its Lord, and the church and the world, which had hitherto walked apart, were soon locked in each other's arms . . . a fatal union."[4]

When Satan couldn't crush the Church, he employed the doctrine of Balaam—he caused it to compromise with the world and dilute its doctrines of truth. It is what Paul warned the Ephesian elders against —wolves coming in to carry believers away from the truth (Acts 20:29-30). Satan will use whatever tactic he can to weaken or destroy God's Church. In the fourth century he did it by Christianizing the Roman Empire and Romanizing the Christian Church.

In short, the Protestant Reformation (1517) was an attempt to break the unholy alliance between the Church and Rome. Fortunately, it was successful in part—today's Protestant churches stand in the tradition of wanting to rid the Church of the doctrines of Balaam and the Nicolaitans. But the price paid by many since the Reformation began has been costly. There is always a price to pay for standing firm in the truth.

The lesson of the church at Pergamos for us is the lesson of Balaam: What you can't curse and crush you can corrupt through compromise. Satan has not given up on that strategy; he is still employing it in today's Church and in Christian families. Wherever two or three are gathered together in Christ's name, Satan will be there to try to corrupt the truth. How is that happening? One word summarizes it: toleration. Christians are supposed to tolerate anyone and anything today while being shoved further to the margins of society. Everything is tolerated except Christianity! The great preacher G. Campbell Morgan summarized the danger of toleration that goes too far:

"There is a toleration which is treachery. There is a peace which issues in paralysis. There are hours when the church must say No to those who ask communion with her, in the doing of her work, upon the basis of compromise. Such standing aloof may produce ostracism and persecution; but it will maintain power and influence. If the church of God in the cities of today were aloof from the maxims of the age, separated from the materialistic philosophies of the schools, bearing witness alone to the all sufficiency of Christ, and the perfection of His salvation, even though persecuted and ostracized and bruised, it would be to her that men would look in the hour of their heartbreak and sorrow and national need. The reason why men do not look to the Church today is that she has destroyed her own influence by compromise."[5]

The Church today has become so fixated on being relevant that it has become irrelevant. We have taken our marching orders from the marketplace and the media instead of from God's Word and have found ourselves out of step with God and His purposes. People in the world find little in local churches that is different from the world. And their attitude is, Why bother?

I would not say that Christians should be combative or antagonistic. But we must speak the truth in love (Ephesians 4:15) wherever corruption or compromise tries to gain a foothold. We do that by being vigilant, sober, and on guard. We remember that Satan prowls around like a lion seeking whom he may devour (1 Peter 5:8). And we remember the lesson from the church at Pergamos. We guard against the dilution of true doctrine by false teaching and authoritarian leaders. If that makes us intolerant in the eyes of some, then so be it. Christ will commend us just as He did Antipas, His "faithful martyr."

Notes:

1. Edwin Yamauchi, *The Archaeology of New Testament Cities in Western Asia Minor* (Grand Rapids, MI: Baker Book House, 1980), 36.
2. Donald Grey Barnhouse, *Revelation: An Expository Commentary* (Grand Rapids, MI: Zondervan, 1971), 51.
3. W. A. Criswell, *Expository Sermons on Revelation* (Grand Rapids, MI: Zondervan, 1962), p. 137.
4. Walter Scott, *Exposition of the Revelation of Jesus Christ* (London, Pickering and Inglis Ltd, ND.) 73.

## APPLICATION

1. As explained in the first three lessons, what does a sword proceeding from the mouth of Christ symbolize? Why is the sword coming from His mouth instead of in His hand? (Revelation 1:16; 2:12, 16)

2. The Greek word for "witness" and "martyr" are the same. What does that say about the boldness of Antipas in Pergamos? (Revelation 2:13)

   a. Why could either English word have been used by Jesus in John 18:37? How did He fulfill both meanings?

   b. What phrase summarizes the responsibility of a witness? (Luke 7:22; John 3:32; Acts 4:20; 22:15; 1 John 1:3)

c. In light of that responsibility, why should we not be afraid of being a witness for Christ? All we have to say is what we have _____ and _____.

d. As mentioned in this lesson, why might it be easier to be faithful to Christ amidst daily persecution than in societies where there is no persecution? How can freedom sometimes breed complacency?

3. Read the account of God's judgment on Israel for intermarrying with the Moabites (Numbers 25). What drastic action stopped the plague? (verses 7-8)

   a. How was Israel to treat those who sought to corrupt the nation? (verses 16-18)

   b. How did Phinehas stand firm for the Lord? (verse 11)

c. What was his reward? (verses 12-13)

d. How can Phinehas be compared with Antipas in Pergamos? (Revelation 2:13)

e. How did Paul act ruthlessly in the case of immorality in the church in Corinth? (1 Corinthians 5:1-5)

f. Why should we be ruthless about corruption or compromise in our own lives? (Galatians 5:9; Ephesians 4:26-27)

g. Take a moment to consider any areas of your life where the "doctrine of Balaam" has been allowed to find a home. (Revelation 2:14)

h. How did this lesson use the Roman Empire under Constantine to illustrate the principle that Satan will use compromise when he cannot outright destroy the Church?

i. How can we create a "Reformation" in our own life when we find compromise or corruption present?

---

**DID YOU KNOW?**

In ancient Greek mythology, snakes were considered sacred sources of healing and wisdom. Supposedly the Greek god Asclepius, in return for some favor, was taught secrets of healing by a snake. In images of Asclepius, his rod is always shown with a snake entwined about it, the snake being associated with healing and with Asclepius, the god of healing. To this day, the snake appears in images associated with modern doctors and healing. And the word scalpel (a knife used in surgery) is derived from "Asclepius." The "Rod of Asclepius" with one intertwined snake is often mistakenly confused with the Caduceus with two intertwined snakes. Some modern healthcare providers use the Rod of Asclepius, some the Caduceus, as a symbol. Common to both is the snake as a symbol of healing going back to Asclepius in Pergamos.

LESSON 5

# THE ADULTEROUS CHURCH: THE LETTER TO THE CHURCH IN THYATIRA

*Revelation 2:18-29*

*In this lesson we discover how even good churches can fall prey to the subtleties of immorality.*

### OUTLINE

There are Christians and churches today who feel a need to be relevant and all-inclusive when it comes to spiritual and moral boundaries. The ancient church in Thyatira must have felt that way as well. This church allowed an immoral individual to lead many others away from Christ.

I. **The Destination of the Letter: Thyatira**

II. **The Designation of the Lord**
   A. The Authority of Jesus
   B. The Awareness of Jesus
   C. The Anger of Jesus

III. **The Diagnosis of the Church**
   A. Thyatira Was a Laboring Church
   B. Thyatira Was a Loving Church
   C. Thyatira Was a Loyal Church
   D. Thyatira Was a Longsuffering Church

IV. **The Denunciation of the Church**

V. **The Declaration to the Church**
   A. The Message to the Cult
   B. The Message to the Christians
   C. The Message to the Conquerors

## OVERVIEW

Something unusual is happening in the Church in America—and I noticed it while visiting England as well in recent years. There are more and more Christians and pastors coming into our two countries than ever before. When I hold meetings with pastors in various American cities, a growing number of them are non-American—they are immigrants who have come to America and England with a missionary vision. They see so many people of their own nationalities living in the West that they want to reach them for Christ.

The obvious question is this: Do these immigrating Christians and leaders not think the Church in the West is capable of reaching the unchurched populations? I regret to say that I don't believe they have that confidence. It's another sign that the Church in the West is in as unstable and ineffective place as I have ever seen it. Yes, there are good things happening in many churches. But as far as a vision for fulfilling the Great Commission and reaching the world in our own communities, we seem to be distracted.

This state of the Church reminds me of the condition of some of the churches to which Christ wrote His seven letters in Revelation 2-3. As I have already said in previous lessons, those churches represented not only their own time-and-place historical situation but they also serve as metaphors for the Church in succeeding historical eras. Some of the problems those first-century churches had have appeared in churches throughout history, even in our own day. We face problems today that Christ addressed in His letters to the seven churches in the apostle John's day.

The church in Ephesus represented the first-century, apostolic church. The church in Smyrna represented the second-and-third-century suffering church in the Roman Empire. And the church in Pergamos represented the compromised and corrupted church under Constantine, beginning in the fourth century. These churches weren't total failures, of course. They had strengths as well as weaknesses. But we are repeating some of the same weaknesses for which Christ corrected the Church centuries ago.

Christ's fourth letter went to the church in Thyatira which suffered from a malady even more modern than the others.

# The Destination of the Letter: Thyatira

Thyatira was located in a valley between Pergamos and Sardis. It had no natural fortifications, its protection coming from a Roman garrison. It was a bustling center of trade, being home to all manner of commercial enterprises. Even though it might be considered the least important of the seven cities to which Christ addressed letters, it received the longest of the seven letters.

The only time Thyatira is mentioned outside the book of Revelation is in Acts 16. Thyatira was the home of a businesswoman named Lydia, a dealer of purple cloth (verse 14). She probably traveled to Philippi on business and, while there, she met the apostle Paul, heard the Gospel, and became a follower of Jesus. It seems likely that she was one of the founders of the church in Philippi. It is also likely that she returned to Thyatira with the Gospel and, in time, established a church in her home city. So the church in Thyatira was probably the "grandchild" of the apostle Paul himself—a strong foundation to say the least.

# The Designation of the Lord (Revelation 2:18)

As with the previous letters, the Lord speaks in a way that reveals His authority, awareness, and anger toward the church in Thyatira.

## *The Authority of Jesus*

Jesus addresses Himself differently to each of the churches. Here He reminds them He has "eyes like a flame of fire, and . . . feet like fine brass." The traits that He reveals about Himself always fit the need of the church in question. The problem in the church in Thyatira was a problem not always in plain sight. But because He has "eyes like a flame of fire," He knows about the problem and can see it plainly. Referring to Himself as "the Son of God" adds seriousness to the situation in the church. The phrase "Son of Man" is more tied to Jesus' humanity, while "Son of God" speaks of His deity.

## *The Awareness of Jesus*

The reference to Jesus' eyes is a reference to His complete awareness; the "flame of fire" refers to His moral judgment. He sees with the exactitude of perfect righteousness. The great commentator J. A. Seiss wrote,

"There is nothing more piercing than flaming fire. Everything yields and melts before it. It penetrates all things, consumes every opposition, sweeps down all obstructions, and presses its way with invincible power. And of this sort are the eyes of Jesus. They look through everything; they pierce through all masks and coverings; they search the remotest recesses; they behold the most hidden things of the soul; and there is no escape from them. As the Son of God He is omniscient as well as almighty."[1]

The disciples of Jesus didn't understand everything about their Master, but one thing they had come to know and believe was that Jesus knew all things (John 16:30; 21:17). The church in Thyatira would not be successful in concealing their sin from Jesus. He reminds them that it is "He who searches the minds and hearts" (Revelation 2:23).

### *The Anger of Jesus*

The final descriptive Jesus gives of Himself is that "His feet [are] like fine brass." In Scripture, brass is a symbol of judgment. This was meant to convey to the church that, not only was He aware of their sin, He was prepared to judge the church for it.

# THE DIAGNOSIS OF THE CHURCH (REVELATION 2:19)

Christ's opening words are full of import: "I know your works, love, service, faith, and your patience; and as for your works, the last are more than the first." There are four commendations from the Lord in those words.

### *Thyatira Was a Laboring Church*

Jesus mentioned their works twice in this opening statement. They were an active church, not a passive one. The word for "service" is the same as the word for "deacon"—those appointed to serve the needs of the local congregation. So they were a working, serving church.

### *Thyatira Was a Loving Church*

Jesus also said, "I know your . . . love." The church in Thyatira was known for its selfless, unconditional love (*agape* in the original language). The church in Ephesus was waning in its *agape* love (Revelation 2:4), but the church in Thyatira was holding steady.

### *Thyatira Was a Loyal Church*

Third, the Lord said, "I know your . . . faith." The Greek word *pistos* can be translated either "faith" or "faithfulness," and they are almost synonymous. People with faith are faithful, meaning they are loyal and dependable. Paul mentioned faithfulness as the chief requirement of servants or stewards, and the believers in Thyatira had that trait (1 Corinthians 4:2).

### *Thyatira Was a Longsuffering Church*

Christ's last commendation for this church was that He knew their "patience." The literal meaning of patience is "staying power under adverse circumstances." When the pain and pressure came, the Christians in Thyatira stood firm. They were "patient in tribulation" as Paul says in Romans 12:12.

One final thought from Christ about this church: "As for your works, the last are more than the first" (verse 19). In other words, they were getting better and stronger. The more they were pressured by the world, the more faithful they became. Their works, love, service, faith, and patience grew stronger all the time. There was *more* (quantitative) and the more was *better* (qualitative). This church deserved Christ's commendation.

But we must remember one thing: Satan doesn't attack bad or weak churches. So Thyatira was a perfect target for Satan's efforts to undermine its ministry.

## THE DENUNCIATION OF THE CHURCH (REVELATION 2:20)

The word "nevertheless" (verse 20) lets us know something is wrong: "Nevertheless, I have a few things against you, because you allow that woman Jezebel, who calls herself a prophetess, to teach and seduce My servants to commit sexual immorality and eat things sacrificed to idols."

John Stott reminds us of Satan's strategy at Thyatira: "If the devil cannot conquer the church by the application of political pressure or the propagation of intellectual heresy, he will try the insinuation of moral evil. This was the dragon's strategy in Thyatira."[2] Holiness was the central thing lacking in the church in Thyatira. She had many good things but she tolerated evil in her midst. The will of God for His people is holiness (Ephesians 1:4; 1 Thessalonians 4:3; Titus 2:13-14).

The reference to the church allowing the presence of Jezebel has Old Testament roots. She was the wife of Ahab, a terribly wicked king of the northern tribes of Israel. Her father was a priest in an idolatrous cult that glorified sexual immorality with temple prostitutes in its worship. Jezebel brought this idolatry into her union with Ahab, king of Israel, who built a temple and altar to the Canaanite goddess Ashtoreth. Jezebel destroyed God's prophets and had 850 of her own false prophets. But King Ahab didn't have the courage to stop his pagan wife. Through the prophet Elijah, God judged Ahab and the wicked and immoral Jezebel (2 Kings 9:33-36).

The spirit of Jezebel had made its way into the church in Thyatira through a female prophetess in the church. She was reviving the immorality of her namesake in the church. For some reason, the leaders of the church were acting like Ahab and not rebuking this prophetess and putting her out of the church. Such are the subtleties of Satan as he worms his way into a church. In spite of her good works, the church in Thyatira was allowing a satanic spirit to introduce immorality.

# THE DECLARATION TO THE CHURCH (REVELATION 2:21-25)

We turn now to what Christ has to say to a church that is tolerating immorality in her midst: a message to the cult, a message to the Christians, and a message to those who would choose to conquer this immorality.

## *The Message to the Cult (Revelation 2:21-23)*

He gives two warnings: to the leader of the cult and to those who have followed her.

1. The Threat of Distress (verse 22a)

Given a chance to repent (verse 21), the prophetess refused. So Christ warned of His judgment: "Indeed I will cast her into a sickbed." If we take that literally, it meant God would strike her with a debilitating disease. (There is a precedent for that in 1 Corinthians 11:29-30.) Figuratively, it might mean that her bed of pleasure would be turned into a bed of pain through some judgment. It doesn't matter how—what matters is that Christ warns of her judgment to come.

I have witnessed situations in which it seemed very obvious that God was disciplining a rebellious Christian; one of those situations led to the untimely death of the person in an "accident." It is not up to us to pass judgment on those situations but to simply take them as warnings. God is holy and will not abide rebellion forever. As Hebrews 10:31 says, "It is a fearful thing to fall into the hands of the living God."

2. The Threat of Death (verse 22b-23a)

The warning was not just to the prophetess but also to "those who commit adultery with her." They would find themselves in "great tribulation" unless they repented of their immorality. Christ promised to "kill her children"—either the physical children born of her immorality or the spiritual children whom she seduced into her practices. Again, it doesn't matter. Either way, Christ was prepared to judge those associated with the immoral prophetess in the church. The story of Ananias and Sapphira shows that God is willing to use death as a judgment in the Church (Acts 5:1-11). The warnings to the church in Thyatira remain warnings to all churches.

## *The Message to the Christians (Revelation 2:24-25)*

Next came Christ's message to the Christians in the church in Thyatira: "But hold fast what you have till I come" (verse 25). These words were for those who had not engaged in the cult of immorality, who had "not known the depths of Satan" (verse 24). There were those who had stood their ground, and Christ exhorts them to stand firm until His return.

There was a group in the church in Thyatira who refused to go along, who refused to take a broad or liberal or enlightened view of doctrine. They knew what God expected and they would not budge. When that happens in today's churches, such people are often looked at as old fashioned, as not with the times. Many Christians today accept practices that would have been unthinkable just a few decades ago. When people learn that I don't drink, don't smoke, and have never been unfaithful to my wife, they almost think I am a dinosaur out of the past. But those are boundaries of life that I have no interest in crossing. And by God's grace I pray I never will. I have simply chosen a path that keeps me from incorporating certain modern practices into my life. If that puts me in a minority in the Body of Christ, so be it. I am happy to be there and to identify with those believers in the church in Thyatira who drew a line in the sand and would not cross over it.

## *The Message to the Conquerors (Revelation 2:26-29)*

The final message is to the conquerors—those who would choose to remain faithful to Christ "until the end" (verse 26). Christ made two promises to this group: they would reign and they would be raptured.

1. The Power to Rule

To the conquerors Christ would "give power over the nations" (verse 26). He quotes from Psalm 2:9, messianic verses that apply specifically to Him: "He shall rule them with a rod of iron; they shall be dashed to pieces like the potter's vessels" (verse 27). They would be given power to rule, Christ said, "as I also have received [power and authority] from My Father" (verse 27). Christ knowingly quoted the messianic verse from Psalms and said those who remained faithful to the end would be given the same power to rule as He was given by the Father.

But rule where and when? This is a specific reference to the millennial reign of Christ. When Christ returns to establish His kingdom on earth, He will bring with Him the faithful of the ages who will rule under His authority for a thousand years (Revelation 17:14; 19:14). The responsibility they will be given during that period will be determined by their faithfulness on earth as followers of Christ. These rewards and responsibilities will be determined at the judgment seat of Christ prior to the Millennium (1 Corinthians 3:11-15). It will pay to have remained faithful to Christ during one's life on earth.

2. The Promise of the Rapture

The final promise is "And I will give him [the conqueror] the morning star" (verse 28). Jesus Christ is the "Bright and Morning Star" (Revelation 22:16). This promise is the gift of Jesus Christ Himself to those who endure and are faithful until His return. The receipt of that gift will happen at the Rapture of the Church when the dead in Christ, and those alive when He returns, will rise from the earth to meet Christ in the clouds (1 Thessalonians 4:15-18). They will dwell in the heavenlies with Christ during the seven-year Tribulation on earth, then return with Him to reign during the Millennium.

One day most of us will fall asleep and be buried on earth, only to be awakened on a day in the future when the Bridegroom returns for His Bride, the Church. Some will be alive on that day! But all who have stood firm until the end will meet the Bright and Morning Star and dwell with Him forever. That is the hope of all who live faithfully in Christ.

Let the warnings and promises of Christ to the church in Thyatira be watchwords for you as you participate in church life in this present day. Satan is alive and well and will do anything He can to keep Christians from remaining faithful until the end.

Notes:

1. Joseph A. Seiss, *The Letters of Jesus: Lenten Lectures* (Philadelphia: Lutheran Bookstore, 1889), 133.
2. John R. W. Stott, *What Christ Thinks Of The Church* (Grand Rapids: Eerdman's Publishing Co., 1958), 72.

## APPLICATION

1. Where did Paul first meet a woman named Lydia? (Acts 16:11-14)

   a. Where was Lydia from? And what was her occupation? (verse 14)

   b. What does the phrase "who worshiped God" suggest about Lydia's spiritual status? (verse 14)

   c. What spiritual progress did she make in her meeting with Paul? (verses 14-15)

   d. She was from Thyatira but also had a house in Philippi. What does that suggest about her means and her influence? (verse 15)

e. Where did Paul and Silas go after being released from jail in Philippi? (verse 40)

f. What might that suggest about Lydia's role in the founding of the church in Philippi?

g. What positive role do homes play in the modern church? What can happen in homes that can't take place in church buildings?

2. In the image of the man who appeared before the prophet Daniel, what were his arms and feet made of? (Daniel 10:2)

a. In Christ's appearance to John the apostle, of what did His feet appear to be made? (Revelation 1:15; 2:18)

b. From verses like 1 Kings 7:30 and 14:27, how strong does it appear bronze (brass) was?

c. Why would bronze (brass) be pictured as the material for arms and feet in human images? What was being conveyed by the choice of that material?

d. What does it suggest about Christ's strength and stability that His feet were pictured as if of bronze (brass)?

3. In Revelation 2:18, "eyes like a flame of fire" have dual importance.
   a. What do eyes signify? (See Luke 12:2-3; 8:17; John 16:30; 21:17.) What does that suggest about the vanity of thinking our acts can be concealed?

b. What does fire signify? (See 1 Corinthians 3:11-15, especially verse 13.) What will the fire of Christ's gaze accomplish at the Judgment Seat of Christ?

4. Could Christ's words—"as for your works, the last are more than the first" (Revelation 2:19b)—apply to you? Is your love, service, faith, and patience greater now than when you first believed?

5. If Satan could empower Jezebel in the ninth century B.C., a prophetess in Thyatira in the first century A.D., could he empower an individual today? How should you therefore live? (1 Peter 5:8)

---
**DID YOU KNOW?**
---

Jezebel, wife of King Ahab of Israel, was the daughter of a priest of the Ashtoreth cult—a Canaanite, pagan cult that worshiped Ashtoreth, an idol-goddess who was the consort of the idol-god Baal. From the time of the Judges on, Israel allowed Baal and Ashtoreth to gain a footing in Israelite religion (Judges 2:11-23). Under the influence of his foreign wives, King Solomon got involved in Ashtoreth worship (1 Kings 11:4-8). For nearly four centuries Ashtoreth and Baal were worshiped in Israel until King Josiah destroyed their centers of worship (2 Kings 23:13-14). In the great confrontation on Mount Carmel, Elijah challenged the prophets of Baal and saw them destroyed (1 Kings 18:16-40).

# LESSON 6

# THE DEAD CHURCH: THE LETTER TO THE CHURCH IN SARDIS

*Revelation 3:1-6*

*In this lesson we discover what can cause a church to die over time.*

## OUTLINE

There are many church buildings in America that are now being used as restaurants, art galleries, or other businesses—even residences! What happened to those churches? The question is, What happened to those churches' members? As the members of a church go, so goes the church.

I. The Destination of the Letter

II. The Designation of the Lord

III. The Denunciation of the Church

IV. The Direction to the Church
   A. Be Sensitive to the Inroads of Sin in the Church
   B. Be Supportive of Those Who Remain True to Christ in the Church
   C. Be Submissive to the Control of the Holy Spirit in the Church
   D. Be Subject to the Authority of God's Word in the Church
   E. Be Sorry and Repent for the Sin of the Church

V. **The Declaration to the Church**
   A. They Shall Be Clothed in White
   B. They Shall Be Continued in the Book
   C. They Shall Be Confessed Before the Father

VI. **The Death of the Church**
   A. We May Rule Out Death From an Outside Enemy
   B. We May Rule Out Death by Suicide
   C. We May Rule Out Death by Abandonment
   D. The Church Died Through the Death of Its Individual Members
   E. The Church Died Because It Relied on Its Past Reputation
   F. The Church Died Because It Let Sin Creep Into the Membership
   G. The Church Died Because It Was Not Sensitive to Its Own Spiritual Condition

## OVERVIEW

Sardis was once one of the world's greatest cities. It sat on a spur of the Tmolus Mountains, surrounded on three sides by huge, impenetrable cliffs. The fourth side was approachable only by an isthmus so narrow that a handful of men could defend it against hundreds. The city was considered impregnable.

Croesus was the greatest king of Sardis, but the city's downfall also happened during his reign. Croesus was arrogant and proud and thought no one could defeat him and his city. But when Croesus and his army met Cyrus the Great and the Persian army, he had to flee for his life back to Sardis. But Croesus was not humbled by this defeat.

For 14 days Cyrus' army lay siege to Sardis. He offered a reward to anyone who could figure out how to get into the city. Observing the city one day, a Persian soldier saw a soldier of Sardis accidentally drop his helmet outside the wall. The Persian soldier was surprised to see the soldier appear at the base of the cliff to retrieve his helmet. So the Persian soldier knew there had to be a passageway into the cliff. That night, the Persian soldier led a group of men to the base of the cliff where they found the crack in the wall. They made their way up the cliff and into Sardis and found it completely unguarded. Croesus thought Sardis was untouchable and did not even bother to have sentries on duty. The Persian soldiers stole through the city and opened the gates, and the Persians captured the city without even a skirmish. The same strategy was used centuries later when another attacking army gained entrance and captured the city.

By the time John wrote Revelation, Sardis was a wealthy but degenerate city. Twice the city had been captured due to arrogance and laziness. Sardis' history is the key to understanding the letter dictated by Christ to John concerning the church in the city. The city's downfall is a metaphor for its spiritual downfall.

## THE DESTINATION OF THE LETTER (REVELATION 3:1)

Sardis means "escaping ones" or "those who come out." In the prophetic view of the Church, Sardis represents the Reformation period (A.D. 1517-1750). That was definitely a period in which many true Christians came out of the Roman church in search of biblical doctrine and practice—leaders like Luther, Knox, Wycliffe, and Zwingli.

# The Designation of the Lord (Revelation 3:1)

Christ introduces Himself with yet another unique descriptive: "He who has the seven Spirits of God and the seven stars." The "seven Spirits" were mentioned in Revelation 1:4 as a reference to the Holy Spirit, seven being the number of perfection. The "seven stars" are clearly explained in Revelation 1:20: "The seven stars are the angels of the seven churches."

# The Denunciation of the Church (Revelation 3:1)

With this church there are no commendations; Christ begins immediately with a denunciation: "I know your works, that you have a name that you are alive, but you are dead." With the previous churches, Christ spoke words of both praise and criticism. Here it is only the latter.

This church had a name and an outward veneer of life. But inwardly, they were dead. The church was full of what we today would call "nominal Christians"—Christians in name only. There are many churches in the world today that bear the name "Christian" but which are filled only with nominal Christians, people in whom the Spirit of God does not live. The church in Sardis was like the "whitewashed tombs" of the Pharisees Jesus spoke about—"beautiful outwardly, but . . . full of dead men's bones" (Matthew 23:27). The church in Sardis was more like a mausoleum than a maternity ward —full of spiritual corpses instead of brimming with new spiritual life.

Charles Swindoll provides a humorous description of a dead church:

"Don't go to that church. It's dead." What exactly does that mean? Maybe it means their sanctuary is a morgue with a steeple. It's a congregation of corpses with undertakers for ushers, embalmers for elders, and morticians for ministers. Their pastor graduated from a theological cemetery. The choir director is the local coroner. They sing "Embalmed in Gilead" and "Amazing Grave, How Sweet the Ground." You might describe their worship as stiff. At the Rapture, they'll be the first churches taken up because the Bible says, "The dead in Christ shall rise first." They drive to church in one long line with their headlights on. Whenever someone joins their membership, the church office immediately notifies the next of kin. Each week they put an ad in the obituaries. The church van is a and the church sign is a tombstone. Their motto is, "Many are cold and a few are frozen."[1]

# THE DIRECTION TO THE CHURCH (REVELATION 3:2-4)

Christ gives five specific exhortations to the church in Sardis.

## Be Sensitive to the Inroads of Sin in the Church (verse 2)

The first exhortation is one found often in Scripture: "Be watchful." The word conveys the idea of "chasing away sleep." In other words, stay awake! Or as the apostle Paul wrote, "Awake, you who sleep, arise from the dead, and Christ will give you light." But it is not just staying awake that is Jesus' point; it is being awake *and* being watchful, a call to perpetual alertness.

I have heard people say, "My church is dying but I feel I should stay and try to keep it alive." I can't argue with such a decision, but you have to make sure you are making a difference in the church instead of the church making a difference in you. If the latter happens, it's time to leave. Some people hate to leave a church which their family attended for generations. But if that church has fallen away from faithfulness to Christ and His Word, then it will ultimately die spiritually if not also physically.

How does death happen? By falling away from doctrine. It's why at my church anyone who teaches in our adult or children's classes must be a member of our church. Why? Because members are required to embrace the doctrinal statement of our church. They have to agree that everything they teach will be in accordance with the Word of God. That may sound restrictive but it's a safeguard to maintain the doctrinal purity of the church. The same gateway applies to all positions of leadership and service in the church: Membership is the door to service. I'm far less concerned with the number of members we have than I am that the members are committed to doctrinal purity.

## Be Supportive of Those Who Remain True to Christ in the Church (verses 2, 4)

The second exhortation is to "strengthen the things which remain, that are ready to die." Verse 4 says that there were "a few names" who had not defiled themselves and who were worthy to be strengthened.

God always preserves a remnant. Before the flood there was Enoch and Noah. In Mesopotamia there was Abraham, and in Sodom there was Lot. God always keeps the light of life burning in some who need to be encouraged to remain faithful. Those who "remain" and have not defiled themselves "shall walk with [Christ] in white, for they are worthy" (verse 4). These will walk with Christ in the New Jerusalem for eternity.

So far, the exhortations are to keep sin on the outside of the church and strengthen the life that remains on the inside.

## *Be Submissive to the Control of the Holy Spirit in the Church (verse 3)*

The third exhortation is to remember: "Remember therefore how you have received and heard" (verse 3). This is a reference to "He who has the seven Spirits of God"—a reference to the Holy Spirit. It is only by the ministry of the Spirit that we hear and receive the Word of God in a life-changing way. When the Spirit leaves, or is grieved or quenched (Ephesians 4:30; 1 Thessalonians 5:19), a church dies. When the human spirit departs, the body dies—and the same is true of a church.

The late John Stott says it well: "We administer great projects and create impressive committees. But we often leave the Holy Spirit out. He has rightly been called the forgotten member of the Trinity. Only when the Church of Christ is filled with the Spirit of Christ can spiritual death be banished and a name for life have any reality behind it."[2]

Worship in a church is a good indicator of the presence of the Spirit. If the worship is vibrant and alive and honoring to God, that's a sign of life. The role of the Spirit is to glorify God, and the church does that through worship. When one of my children was in college and trying to find a church to attend, he would call home with discouraging reports. One church had great worship but no biblical preaching; another church would have preaching but dead worship. Where the Holy Spirit is alive and working, a church will have both.

## *Be Subject to the Authority of God's Word in the Church (verse 3)*

"Hold fast" is the fourth exhortation. "Hold fast" (literally, "keep") in Scripture is usually an exhortation tied to remaining faithful to the Word of God. "Keeping" the Word of God is a theme throughout the book of Revelation (Revelation 1:3; 3:8; 12:17; 22:7).

Keeping the Word of God means to obey it and remain true to it. If a church keeps the Word, it means the Bible will be honored and taught faithfully. When a church abandons the Bible, it removes the Holy Spirit's chief means of transforming believers into the image of Christ.

One of my seminary professors, Dr. Bruce Waltke, was once invited to speak to an adult Sunday school class in a mainline denominational church. When he realized none of the members of the class had Bibles, he asked if Bibles could be provided. The class was delayed for quite some time while a search was made for Bibles. When a box of Bibles was discovered in a storage closet, Dr. Waltke was able to proceed with his lesson. That was not a church that was keeping the Word of God.

### *Be Sorry and Repent for the Sin of the Church (verse 3)*

The previous exhortation and this final one are linked together: "Hold fast and repent." This is the same exhortation (to repent) given to the churches in Ephesus (Revelation 2:5) and Pergamos (Revelation 2:16). God's plan for recovery is always the same: repent. Change your mind, turn around, and go back to the baseline of truth—the Word of God. Churches can only do that when individual members do it. It is an exhortation to a church, but it begins with individual members.

## THE DECLARATION TO THE CHURCH (REVELATION 3:5-6)

If the church in Sardis does what Christ exhorts them to do, there will be a threefold promise that God will fulfill: eternal life.

### *They Shall Be Clothed in White (verse 5)*

Revelation 19:8b says that the "clean and bright" linen worn by the saints who return with Christ stands for "the righteous acts of the saints." In Roman culture, the "Day of Triumph" was observed by Roman citizens donning a white toga in order to be honored by civic authorities. This is the image of walking with Christ "in white"—a triumphant procession leading to eternal life.

### *They Shall Be Continued in the Book (verse 5)*

Their names will remain in "the Book of Life." Again, in Roman times a register was kept, like our modern census, of the names of the citizens of a city. If a citizen acted in an unlawful or dishonorable way, his name was erased from the registry. Noble acts resulted in a name being written in gold letters. So the image is that those who are faithful to Christ will never have their names blotted out of the Book of Life. Jesus encouraged His followers to rejoice that their names were "written in heaven" (Luke 10:20).

### *They Shall Be Confessed Before the Father (verse 5)*

Another promise: "I will confess his name before My Father and before His angels." The cultural image is of honored citizens or soldiers being processed before the emperor and having their names read out along with the record of their valor and deeds. In the same way, those who have been faithful to Christ will be presented before the Father and their names confessed before Him.

## THE DEATH OF THE CHURCH

Let us do a spiritual autopsy of the church in Sardis to determine how it died.

### *We May Rule Out Death From an Outside Enemy*

We know from the history of the Church that all attempts to crush it have failed. Every time someone has tried to stamp out the Church of Jesus Christ, it has resulted in even further and more committed growth. The Romans, the Nazis, the Communists—all have failed to eradicate the Church when they have tried. The church in Sardis did not die from external sources.

### *We May Rule Out Death by Suicide*

The church in Sardis did not die on purpose; it did not die intentionally by some premeditated cause. No one said, "Let's destroy our church and abandon our faith in Christ." They didn't call a meeting, draw up a resolution, and declare themselves no longer interested in following Christ. I suppose a church could die that way, but that would happen quickly. Churches like the church in Sardis die over time, not overnight.

### *We May Rule Out Death by Abandonment*

The church was not abandoned by faithful Christians or by God. We have already learned that there was a remnant of committed believers still in the church that remained committed to Christ.

They may have been surrounded by dead or nominal Christians, but the remnant had not abandoned them.

If the church didn't die at the hands of an enemy, by suicide, or by abandonment, how did it die? There were four causes of its death.

## *The Church Died Through the Death of Its Individual Members*

I have previously noted that a church or a nation is just a collection of individuals. If a church, family, nation, or other organization dies, it is because of its members. As the parts go, so goes the whole. Churches die one member at a time, little by little. If a church is alive, it is because its members are vibrant and alive.

Consider the story of the pastor who told his congregation he was going to preach the funeral service of their dying church. But he wanted the members to come forward and witness the deceased in the casket he had arranged in the front of the church. As the members filed by and peered into the casket they saw a reflection of themselves in the mirror the pastor had placed in the casket. The members got the point: If the church is dying, it's because the members are dying individually.

## *The Church Died Because It Relied on Its Past Reputation*

The city of Sardis itself was captured because it rested on its tradition of being impregnable. It was arrogant and prideful. It had become a monument to its past glory. The same was true of the church in Sardis which had once been alive. But they grew content and complacent and self-satisfied. They drifted into spiritual unconsciousness and the church died.

The church was taken captive by pride the way the city was captured by Persia. Being overly dependent on past success is a recipe for death.

## *The Church Died Because It Let Sin Creep Into the Membership*

Herodotus, the Greek historian, recorded that the church in Sardis had a reputation for lax moral standards and even open sin in the church. There can be no secret sin since all is seen by the eyes of Christ. If there is unconfessed and unrepentant sin, the Spirit will depart.

## The Church Died Because It Was Not Sensitive to Its Own Spiritual Condition

Simply put, the church of Sardis failed to follow the principle of 1 Corinthians 11:31: "For if we would judge ourselves, we would not be judged."

Let us hear what the Spirit says to the churches! (Revelation 3:6)

Notes:

1. Charles Swindoll, *Insights on Revelation* (Grand Rapids, MI: Zondervan, 2011), Kindle Edition.
2. John R. W. Stott, *What Christ Thinks of the Church* (Grand Rapids: Wm. B. Eerdmans Publishing Co., 1958), 98.

## APPLICATION

1. In Matthew 23, Jesus pointed out eight different kinds of religious hypocrisy. Identify each reason He criticized the Pharisees:

    a. verse 13

    b. verse 14 (not found in some translations)

    c. verse 15

    d. verse 16

    e. verse 23

    f. verse 25

    g. verse 27

    h. verse 29

i. Explain the significance of "whitewashed tombs" in verses 27-28. How could that metaphor be applied to an individual as well as a group or church?

j. How did this lesson apply this metaphor to the church in Sardis?

k. In what sense were the Pharisees (like the Sardis church) guilty of building on their traditions and status instead of on true spirituality?

2. Read Ephesians 4:25-32.

   a. What is the key principle as given in verse 30?

b. List all the ways Paul suggests the Spirit can be grieved (verses 25-29, 31).

c. What kind of behavior can we assume, by contrast, does not grieve the Holy Spirit? (verse 32).

3. What metaphor for the Spirit's life in the Church does Paul use in 1 Thessalonians 5:19?

a. What evidences does Paul give for the presence of the Spirit in the Church? (verses 16-18, 20-22)

b. Why is verse 21 a key principle in determining what is of the Spirit and what is not?

c. What is the measure by which all spiritual activity must be tested? (Acts 17:11)

d. Why is prayerful discernment needed? (2 Corinthians 11:13-15)

4. The early church began to be persecuted externally in Jerusalem in Acts 3. Record what happened to the church subsequently:

   a. Acts 4:4

   b. Acts 5:14

c. Acts 6:1


d. Acts 6:7


e. Acts 9:31


f. Acts 9:35, 42


g. Acts 11:21, 24


h. Acts 14:1


i. Acts 14:21


j. Why is Matthew 16:18 proof that the Church can never be destroyed externally?

5. Why would the church in Sardis have been wise to heed the words of 1 Corinthians 10:12?

6. The life or death of a church depends on the life or death of its

   _____.

---

### DID YOU KNOW?

The Protestant Reformation began in A. D. 1517 and lasted until around 1750. The primary action of the Roman church that prompted the Reformation was the sale of indulgences—church decrees purchased by church members that guaranteed the release of deceased persons from Purgatory. There were many other abuses of biblical spirituality, but Martin Luther, a German monk, was incensed by the unbiblical practice of the sale of indulgences. On October 31, 1517, Luther nailed his now-famous "95 Theses"—complaints against the Roman church—to the door of the church in Wittenberg, Germany. The church persecuted Luther and he was forced to go into hiding. But he survived and was joined by many other scholars and leaders who left the Roman church in pursuit of biblical Christianity.

# LESSON 7

# THE FAITHFUL CHURCH: THE LETTER TO THE CHURCH IN PHILADELPHIA

*Revelation 3:7-13*

*In this lesson we learn the reasons Christ had only good things to say about a particular church.*

## OUTLINE

Modern church life has become very complicated and multi-faceted. But for a first-century church that Christ spoke highly of, life was basic and principled. Christ commended them for three things—principles that can be lost among the practices and programs of the modern church.

I. The Destination of the Letter

II. The Designation of the Lord
    A. Jesus Is Holy
    B. Jesus Is Genuine
    C. Jesus Is Sovereign

III. The Diagnosis of the Lord
    A. They Have an Open Door
    B. They Have a Little Strength
    C. They Have Kept the Word of God
    D. They Have Not Denied the Lord

IV. The Declaration of Christ to the Church
    A. He Promises to Humiliate Their Enemies
    B. He Promises to Keep Them From the Hour of Trial
    C. He Promises to Come Quickly

V. The Direction for Us
    A. The Potential of the Local Church
    B. The People of the Local Church
    C. The Principles of the Local Church
    D. The Priorities of the Local Church

## OVERVIEW

If I could have been at any one of the seven churches on the day Christ's letter arrived, I would have chosen the church in Philadelphia. This church is the only one, besides the letter to the church in Smyrna, to which Christ had nothing negative to say. In this lesson we will discover why our Lord commended this church in such an encouraging manner.

## THE DESTINATION OF THE LETTER

The ancient city of Philadelphia is on the site of the modern city of Alysr in Turkey. It was named after Attalus Philadelphus, king of Pergamon. "Philadelphia" is best known today for its original Greek meaning "brotherly love." Besides occurring as the name of a city, the Greek word occurs several times in the New Testament referring to love and affection between Christians.

From a prophetic perspective, the church in Philadelphia represents the universal Church from the beginning of the nineteenth century to the Rapture of the Church, overlapping with the period of the church in Laodicea. Thinking positively, the Philadelphia church represents the modern age of the spread of the Gospel around the world.

## THE DESIGNATION OF THE LORD (REVELATION 3:7)

As He did in all six previous letters, Christ begins by describing Himself in terms of an attribute: "These things says He who is holy, He who is true, 'He who has the key of David, He who opens and no one shuts, and shuts and no one opens.'"

### *Jesus Is Holy*

"Holy" in Scripture meant to be set apart for a unique use—specifically, to be set apart for God. So Christ is the Holy One in the sense of the "only one," the only begotten Son of God (John 3:16). Peter tells us that since He who has called us is holy, we ourselves should be holy as well (1 Peter 1:15). Because Christ is holy He has the right to call His Church to be holy as well.

### *Jesus Is Genuine*

He is also "true"—a reference to Christ's genuineness. He was not only holy, set apart without sin wholly unto God, but He was true, genuine, and full of integrity. As He said in John 14:6, "I am the . . . truth." Jesus does not spin His words as so often happens in the modern media. His Yes is Yes and His No is No (Matthew 5:37).

### *Jesus Is Sovereign*

Christ's sovereignty is revealed by His having "the key of David" and being the One who can open and shut by His own will. The key of David refers to a man in the Old Testament named Eliakim who carried "the key of the house of David" (Isaiah 22:22). He had authority over the treasures of the king and the power to open and shut the door at will. This reference from the Old Testament is used by Christ to describe His own authority. That is a message of sovereign authority and power that Christ is communicating to the church in Philadelphia.

## THE DIAGNOSIS OF THE LORD (REVELATION 3:8)

Any modern church that wants to receive the Lord's commendation could benefit by knowing the four ways Christ commended the church in Philadelphia.

### *They Have an Open Door*

Remember Christ's words of introduction about Himself, that He has the key by which to open and close doors. With that in mind, He tells the church in Philadelphia, "I have set before you an open door, and no one can shut it."

The notion of an open door appears several times in the New Testament. Paul talked about a door for ministry that was open for him in Ephesus (1 Corinthians 16:8-9). He said the same thing about his opportunity for ministry in Troas (2 Corinthians 2:12). And in Colossians 4:2-3, Paul talked about praying "that God would open to us a door for the word, to speak the mystery of Christ." In each case, the "open door" represents an opportunity for ministry. That would include people on the other side of the door who were receptive to Paul's message. Sometimes doors are open and sometimes they are not.

This metaphor of an open door had particular relevance to the Philadelphia church as explained by the great historian Sir William Ramsay:

"The situation of the city fully explains this saying. Philadelphia lay at the upper extremity of a long valley which opens back from the sea. After passing Philadelphia, the road along this valley ascends to the Phrygian land and the great central plateau and the main mass of Asia Minor. This road was the one which led from the harbor of Smyrna to the northeastern parts of Asia Minor and the east in general and the one rival to the great route connecting Ephesus to the east and the great Asian trade route of Medieval times. Philadelphia therefore was the keeper of the gateway to the plateau."[1]

Philadelphia was a gateway city to a large region that included other cities. Christ was reminding the church in Philadelphia that they were in a strategic location for ministry because of their location.

And the late John Stott of England adds great discernment to the notion of open doors for ministry:

"Christ has the keys and He opens the doors. Then let us not barge our way unceremoniously through doors which are still closed. We must wait for Him to make openings for us. Damage is continually being done to the cause of Christ by rude or blatant testimony. It is indeed right to seek to win for Christ our friends and relatives at home and at work, but we are sometimes in a greater hurry than God is. Be patient, pray hard, love much, and wait expectantly for the opportunity of witness. The same applies to our future. More mistakes are probably made by speed than by sloth, by impatience than by deleteriousness. God's purposes often ripen slowly and if the door is shut, don't put your shoulder to it. Wait till Christ takes out the key and opens it up."[2]

The church in Philadelphia is reminded by Christ that He is able to open doors for ministry that no one can close. And the same is true for every church today that will pray for Him to open doors for it. The Philadelphian age of the Church is the age of the open door.

## *They Have a Little Strength*

Christ next makes a rather strange sounding commendation. He has just reminded them of His opening for them a great opportunity, but then says "you have a little strength." What did He mean?

Literally, the Greek text conveys this idea: You have "but little strength." Christ presents their situation as almost problematic: You have a *big* opportunity but only a *little* strength. The obvious implication is that it is not their strength that is important but Christ's strength. This brings to mind Christ's words to Paul: "My strength is made perfect in weakness" (2 Corinthians 12:9). Paul learned that in His weakness, Christ's strength was more than sufficient. That is the message of Christ for His Church in all places and in all ages. What we do in our strength has no staying power, but what Christ does for us in His strength will last for eternity.

### *They Have Kept the Word of God*

Third, Christ commends the church in Philadelphia for their fidelity to the Word of God: "[You] have kept My Word."

When I did scores of radio interviews after my book, *I Never Thought I'd See the Day!* was published, the question I was asked most often was this: "What is the one thing that is most responsible for erosion of biblical standards in the Church?" I didn't need to think for long about that answer—it is the removal of the Word of God from the pulpits of churches. When Christians don't know what God's desires and standards are, how can they keep them? And how can they keep from being conformed to the world when the world violates God's standards? They can't!

One of the reasons the church in Philadelphia was blessed by God was because of their faithfulness to His Word.

### *They Have Not Denied the Lord*

Finally, Christ commended the church in Philadelphia because they had not denied His name. They were faithful not only to the Word of the Lord but to the Lord Himself. They would not participate in the Caesar worship that was so common in their day. Even in the face of persecution they would not deny the name of Christ.

If we want to be commended by Christ like the church of Philadelphia, we will go through open doors of ministry, depend on His strength, and be true to Him and to His Word.

# THE DECLARATION OF CHRIST TO THE CHURCH (REVELATION 3:9-13)

Christ then makes three declarations to the church in Philadelphia.

### *He Promises to Humiliate Their Enemies (verse 9)*

The same group that attacked the church in Smyrna was attacking the church in Philadelphia: Jews who claimed to be serving God under false pretenses; Jews who were not really Jews in the true spiritual sense but were false apostles. Jesus referred to them in Smyrna and Philadelphia as "the synagogue of Satan." But Christ says He will humiliate them: "Indeed I will make them come and worship before your feet, and to know that I have loved you." Just as Christ humiliated Paul on the road to Damascus, so He will humiliate those attacking the church in Philadelphia.

We do not have to fight our own spiritual battles when we are attacked for following Christ. He is sufficient to defend us from all our enemies.

## *He Promises to Keep Them From the Hour of Trial (verse 10)*

This next promise of Christ—"I also will keep you from the hour of trial which shall come upon the whole world, to test those who dwell on the earth"—is one of the most important in the New Testament.

When we study the book of Revelation, we find the Church mentioned in chapters 1-4 but never again. It's as if the Church vanishes from John's vision after chapter four. That makes sense because the rest of Revelation is about the Tribulation from which the Church will be spared. While there is tribulation on earth the Church is in heaven with Christ—and Revelation 3:10 is the promise that explains the Church's absence. This promise is not to spare the church in Philadelphia from some local or regional persecution. The trial they will avoid will "come upon the whole world." It is a universal time of testing from which the Philadelphia church will be spared.

"Hour of trial" can be translated "hour of testing." It is a reference to the seven-year Tribulation that will precede Christ's Second Coming. And from a prophetic perspective, this promise to the church in Philadelphia means the Church on earth seven years prior to Christ's return will be kept from that "hour of trial." Not kept *through* the hour of trial, but kept *from* the hour of trial. Some believe the Church will go through the Tribulation and be preserved *through* it. But that is not what the text says: "from the hour of trial." The Rapture (removal from earth) of the Church is the means by which God will keep the Church *from* the hour of trial (Romans 8:1a; 1 Thessalonians 4:16-17).

## *He Promises to Come Quickly (verses 11-12a)*

The promise is that Christ will come quickly: "Behold, I am coming quickly! Hold fast what you have, that no one may take your crown. He who overcomes, I will make him a pillar in the temple of My God."

"Quickly" doesn't mean immediately as we think of time. "Quickly" refers not to *when* He will come but *how* He will come: "in a moment, in the twinkling of an eye, at the last trumpet" (1 Corinthians 15:52a). It will happen quickly, in a moment of time.

# THE DIRECTION FOR US

There are five ways the modern Church can gain direction from the church in Philadelphia.

## *The Potential of the Local Church*

The Philadelphian church was a church of opportunity, and so is every local church in the world. If Christ is present and the church is committed to Him, I believe He wants to put before that church a door of opportunity for ministry. Therefore, every church should pray for those doors to be recognized, opened, and walked through to discover the opportunities God has ordained. Churches too often focus on their limitations and problems—what they perceive as closed doors. Instead, churches should assume that God has called them to the place and given them the resources they need to walk through open doors. Every church's open doors will be different, but every church has them.

## *The People of the Local Church*

What we consider a weakness in the local church—there are too few people, we have too little money, we have too few gifts, we have too few opportunities—Christ sees as a strength. Remember: When we are weak or little, Christ is strong and big. He commended the Philadelphian church for having "little strength" because that meant the church would have to depend on Him. Being humanly weak is not to be despised (Zechariah 4:10). Building the Church of Jesus Christ is not up to us. We depend on the head of the Church to give His Body the strength we need. When we perceive ourselves as having little strength, we are exactly where we need to be for Christ to reveal His strength in us.

## *The Principles of the Local Church*

In one verse (verse 8) Christ summarizes three principles that apply to every Church: open doors for ministry, depending on Christ's strength, and keeping the Word of God. The third one—being faithful to God's Word—will lead to the first two since they are both taught in the Bible. The greatest tragedy in the modern Church is the failure to faithfully teach the whole counsel of God as found in Scripture. Teaching and applying the Bible's truths will lead us to fulfill every other priority God has for the local church.

# *The Priorities of the Local Church*

The Church of Jesus Christ is *His* Church. That means boldly identifying with Christ regardless of the cost. The church in Philadelphia was commended by Christ because they had not denied His name. The Bible is Christ's book. Jesus was faithful to the precepts of the Word of God and He expects us to be as well.

When we are asked by the world (as the Philadelphians were asked by the Romans), "Do you believe Christ is God? Do you worship Christ and none other? Are you willing to die for your faith in Christ?" . . . . If the answer to those questions is Yes, then we are not denying His name. If our answers about Christ are in any way different from the Bible's answers about Christ, then we are denying His name. The top priority of every church that calls itself Christian is to lift up and exalt the name of the One we say is Lord and Savior. It is not enough to proclaim Christ as "moral example" or "great teacher" (though He was those, and more). We must proclaim Christ as the Bible does—the only name whereby we can be saved (Acts 4:12).

God blesses Christ and His Word regardless of the motivations of the preacher or the church. Remember that when Paul was in prison he rejoiced that other self-serving leaders were trying to take his place. Paul didn't care about their motivations. He cared only that the Gospel of Christ was being preached (Philippians 1:12-18). That remains my only priority for the church I pastor and for the ministry I conduct. I know God will bless the work of any church or ministry that keeps Christ and His Gospel their main priority.

The church in Philadelphia was a church commended by Christ for many reasons. Our goal should be to model our churches after theirs, beginning with every individual member. Let your church's faithfulness begin with you.

Notes:

1. Sir William Mitchell Ramsay, *The Letters to the Seven Churches of Asia* (London: Hodder and Stoughton, 1906), 404.
2. John Stott, *What Christ Thinks of the Church* (Grand Rapids, MI: Eerdmans, 1972), 111.

## APPLICATION

1. How is the Greek word *philadelphia* translated in each of the following verses (see the first paragraph in this lesson)?

    a. Romans 12:10

    b. 1 Thessalonians 4:9

    c. Hebrews 13:1

    d. 1 Peter 1:22

    e. 2 Peter 1:7 (two occurrences)

    f. The primary Greek word for love, *agape*, means "unconditional, sacrificial love." How would you contrast *agape* and *philadelphia*?

    g. Which is more feeling-based? Which is more an act of the will?

2. Read 1 Peter 1:13-16.

   a. What connection is there between Christ's holiness (Revelation 3:7) and our holiness? (verses 15-16)

   b. Holiness conveys the idea of separateness. How is that idea captured in verse 14?

   c. How is that idea conveyed by Paul in 2 Corinthians 6:17?

   d. What would a "holy" Christian look like in today's world? What does it mean to "come out and be separate"?

   e. How does John 5:30 convey Christ's strategy for being holy while on earth? How can we live the same way?

3. Jesus said, "I am the way, the _____ , and the life." (John 14:6)

   a. Quoting Psalm 119:160, what else did Jesus say was truth? (John 17:17)

b. What did John call Jesus in John 1:1?

c. So the Bible is the_____ Word of God and Jesus is

   the_____ Word of God. And both are_____.

4. Describe the references to "doors" made by Paul in the following verses:

   a. 1 Corinthians 16:8-9

   b. 2 Corinthians 2:12

   c. Colossians 4:2-3

   d. How should we determine whether an opportunity is actually a door being opened by God?

e. Describe the process Paul went through in finding an opportunity for ministry in Acts 16:6-10. (Note the word "concluding" in verse 10.)

5. Using Isaiah 22:22 as background, Christ identifies Himself as having "the key of David" in Revelation 3:7. Are the keys He gave to Peter the same? Why or why not? (Matthew 16:19)

6. Explain the importance of "keep you from," contrasted with "keep you through," in Revelation 3:10. Are you glad it says "from" instead of "through"? Explain.

---

**DID YOU KNOW?**

---

Revelation 3:10 is a verse at the core of how one views the Church and the Tribulation. Bible students who take that verse at face value are *pretribulational*—believing the Rapture will occur before the Tribulation begins. Students who believe the Church will go through the Tribulation (but be protected) are *posttribulational*—believing the Rapture of the Church and the Second Coming happen at the same time at the end of the Tribulation. There are some who take a mediating view: The Church will be spared the most intense part of the Tribulation only, the second three-and-a-half years. They are *midtribulationalists*, believing the Rapture will occur midway through the Tribulation.

# LESSON 8

# THE DISGUSTING CHURCH: THE LETTER TO THE CHURCH IN LAODICEA

*Revelation 3:14-22*

*In this lesson we discover Christ's message to the Church that exists at the end of this age.*

## OUTLINE

There are a few places in Scripture where God uses harsh language to address His people. Nowhere is such language harsher than in Christ's words to the church in Laodicea—a church that made Him sick. Today's Church should take note; those words may apply to us as well.

I. **The Correspondent to the Last Age Church**
   A. Jesus Is the Confirmation of the Word
   B. Jesus Is the Creator of the World

II. **The Characteristics of the Last Age Church**
   A. The Laodicean Church Is a Compromising Church
   B. The Laodicean Church Is a Conceited Church
   C. The Laodicean Church Is a Christless Church

III. **The Counsel to the Last Age Church**
   A. The Prescription for Spiritual Poverty
   B. The Prescription for Spiritual Nakedness
   C. The Prescription for Spiritual Blindness
   D. The Prescription for Spiritual Compromise
   E. The Prescription for Their Christlessness

## OVERVIEW

As I travel around preaching the Word of God, I notice that many churches have Sunday school classes named after churches or people mentioned in the Bible. There might be a class called the Bereans, or the Philadelphia class, or the Ephesians. But so far, I have never encountered a church or class named after the Laodicean church. The reason for that will be apparent when we read what Christ said about the church in Laodicea in Asia Minor.

Christ's letter to the Laodiceans is the only one of the seven letters that says nothing positive about the church to which it is addressed. In fact, this church made Christ "sick" in a manner of speaking.

The city of Laodicea was wealthy due to the production of wool fabric. As a result, the church was well off; but its members' material prosperity had lulled the church to sleep. The church in Laodicea was the last of the seven churches Christ addressed. From a prophetic perspective the church represents the universal Church at the end of the age before Christ returns to earth. The church in Laodicea is a sobering wake-up call for us who realize we may be living in the age represented by this apathetic church. It means Christ has little to commend the Church that will exist when He returns.

The church in Laodicea—and by extension, the modern church—failed to point people to Christ as the way of eternal salvation. It had become a lukewarm social organization instead of a lighthouse pointing people to safety in Christ. As we read about this church we have to ask ourselves whether we are like the Christians in Laodicea.

# THE CORRESPONDENT TO THE LAST AGE CHURCH (REVELATION 3:14)

As with all the letters, Christ identifies Himself as He begins to speak. This time, He is the confirmation of the Word and the creator of the world.

### Jesus Is the Confirmation of the Word (Revelation 3:14b)

"These things says the Amen, the Faithful and True Witness"—the description Christ gives of Himself. As with the other letters, Christ's self-description addresses the particular church. Naming Himself as "Faithful and True" stands in direct contrast to the unfaithfulness and deceit of the church in Laodicea. In short, "Amen" means integrity.

When Jesus calls Himself "the Amen," it is the same as His words in John 14:6: "I am the . . . truth." Jesus is God's confirmation of all that God is.

### *Jesus Is the Creator of the World (Revelation 3:14c)*

Jesus is also "the Beginning of the creation of God." That doesn't mean Jesus was the first part of God's creation since He has always existed (John 1:1-2). Rather, it means Jesus is the source of creation (John 1:3; Colossians 1:16; Hebrews 1:2). Christ wants the Laodiceans to remember that everything they have came through Him. They are not in control; Jesus is in control as the Source of all creation. Every good and perfect gift comes from above, not from below (James 1:17).

# THE CHARACTERISTICS OF THE LAST AGE CHURCH (REVELATION 3:15-17, 20)

The church in Laodicea was lacking in every way. It was a compromising, conceited, and Christless church. The modern church, unfortunately, bears many of those same marks.

### *The Laodicean Church Is a Compromising Church (Revelation 3:15-16)*

The compromising nature of the church is revealed in Christ's famous words that the church was "neither cold nor hot." They couldn't take a stand on anything. Because they wouldn't, Christ said, "I will vomit you out of My mouth."

This is the only place where the Greek word for "lukewarm, tepid" is used. And it is a reference to mineral springs surrounding Laodicea. The mineral springs outside the city were hot; but by the time the water reached the city via conduits, it would have cooled slightly. It would be lukewarm instead of hot. The same was true, only in reverse, for cold water piped to Laodicea from Colossae. It would be lukewarm by the time it arrived. Whether it started hot or cold, by the time the water reached Laodicea it was lukewarm.

Jesus used the lukewarm waters of Laodicea to illustrate the hearts of the Christians there. He said, "I could wish you were cold or hot"—at least they would know what they did or didn't believe. But to be lukewarm is a "go along to get along" mentality, a willingness to blend in with whatever crowd you are with. It happens to lots of Christians—they start off hot for Christ but over time become lukewarm. A lukewarm Christian is one ripe for compromise.

## *The Laodicean Church Is a Conceited Church (Revelation 3:17)*

The Laodicean Christians had a high view of themselves. They said, "I am rich, have become wealthy, and have need of nothing." But Christ gave them a reality check: "[You] do not know that you are wretched, miserable, poor, blind, and naked." God measures things differently than man does.

Dr. John Walvoord gives a good picture of the church in Laodicea:

"The church at Laodicea with their unconscious need were lulled into false contentment by their temporal sufficiency. Spiritually they were in a wretched state but did not realize it. Without the real joy of the Lord, they were miserable in spite of their temporal wealth. They were poor because they were without real and eternal possessions and were lacking the eye of faith that could ascertain the true riches which endure forever. They were blind to things which could be seen only by spiritual sight, and they were naked of spiritual clothing, the righteousness which comes from God, even though they were clothed with rich garments of silk and wool. The Laodiceans are typical of the modern world, which revels in that which the natural eye can see but is untouched by the gospel and does not see beyond the veil of the material to the unseen and real eternal spiritual riches."[1]

It's a shame that the church in Europe, the birthplace of the Protestant Reformation, is a mere shadow of its former self. It has lost all true spiritual power and authority; many churches have closed, and those that exist have mostly small attendance. Will that happen in America? It could if we deceive ourselves into thinking that we are "wealthy, and have need of nothing." If we attract people to our churches for the wrong reasons they will never grow into strong, mature Christians. We cannot use the world's methods and the world's measuring stick to gauge the health or success of the modern Church. If we do, Christ will say to us what He said to Laodicea.

## *The Laodicean Church Is a Christless Church (Revelation 3:20)*

Revelation 3:20 is a classic verse used in personal evangelism: "Behold, I stand at the door and knock. If anyone hears My voice and opens the door, I will come in to him and dine with him, and he with Me." Christ is standing outside the Laodicean church trying to gain entrance. He is knocking on the door hoping someone will answer and let Him in.

Beyond personal evangelism, think of the prophetic significance of this verse for the Church in the last days: Christ is trying to gain access to His own Church to be its Lord! It is a picture of what Christ said in Luke 18:8: "Nevertheless, when the Son of Man comes, will He really find faith on the earth?" What a terrible characterization of the Church in the last days!

# THE COUNSEL TO THE LAST AGE CHURCH (REVELATION 3:18-21)

Christ gave five-part counsel to the sickly church in Laodicea. Because this church represents the age in which we live, we would be well advised to apply this counsel to our lives and churches today.

## *The Prescription for Spiritual Poverty (Revelation 3:18a)*

The first piece of counsel is filled with irony: "I counsel you to buy from Me gold refined in the fire, that you may be rich." The irony is that the Laodiceans considered themselves to be rich, and they were. But their riches were worldly, not spiritual. Their money was useless for what they really needed—spiritual healing and maturity. They needed spiritual wealth which can only come through Christ. The gold they needed was the kind refined in the fire of suffering and obedience. The Laodiceans could have those riches but at a price.

The Bible addresses money and wealth as much as any other topic. Paul wrote to Timothy to tell wealthy members of the church in Ephesus to be "rich in good works, ready to give, willing to share, storing up for themselves a good foundation for the time to come, that they may lay hold on eternal life" (1 Timothy 6:18-19). There was no condemnation of wealth, just the exhortation to be generous with it as a channel of blessing through good works.

I have found through the years that God has blessed many Christians with amazing wealth. These people are often looking for godly ways to use their money. Those of us who don't have outsized wealth don't realize that being a steward of that money is difficult. Knowing how and where to use it requires a commitment to wisdom and discernment. Most people think life would be easier with great wealth, but a Christian with wealth bears a burden of responsibility to discover God's purpose in blessing him with that wealth—and to use it accordingly. That discovery begins with realizing that true wealth comes through the riches of knowing Christ.

## *The Prescription for Spiritual Nakedness (Revelation 3:18b)*

Not only was the church in Laodicea spiritually poor, they were spiritually naked as well (verse 17). So Christ's next words of counsel are that they acquire from Him "white garments, that [they] may be clothed, that the shame of [their] nakedness may not be revealed."

The Laodiceans' condition reminds us of the story by Hans Christian Andersen, "The Emperor's New Clothes." A weaver pretended to create a suit of clothes that would be invisible to those unworthy to hold their positions, all of whom didn't dare to say that the king was wearing no clothes—until a shameless child cried out, saying the king wasn't wearing anything! The Laodiceans pretended to be clothed in righteousness, but in fact they were naked. And nobody had the nerve to say so until Christ, the Lord of the Church, pointed out their nakedness to them. Nakedness in Scripture is a metaphor for defeat and humiliation, and that was the condition of the Laodicean church. Christ's counsel is to procure "white garments" from Him that the shame of their nakedness might be covered.

White raiment is defined later in Revelation 19:8—the clothing worn by the saints who return with Christ at His Second Coming: "for the fine linen is the righteous acts of the saints." The Laodicean believers had no white garments to wear because they had no righteous acts. Their lukewarm approach to obedience, generosity, and service left them naked in the eyes of God. When Christians are "on fire" (that is, hot instead of lukewarm) for the Lord, the natural result will be the good works for which they were saved (Ephesians 2:10). Instead of being hot, their tepid approach to true spirituality produced no fruit and no covering of white garments of righteousness.

## *The Prescription for Spiritual Blindness (Revelation 3:18c)*

Christ noted that the Laodiceans were "blind" (verse 17), and He has counsel for their condition: "anoint your eyes with eye salve, that you may see." This was another culturally relevant reference—Laodicea was famous for its export of a powder (tephra Phrygia—powder of Phrygia) that, mixed with water, created an eye salve. It supposedly did have some medicinal benefit. So while they knew how to tend to physical eye problems, they were completely blind when it came to seeing spiritual things.

Spiritual blindness is a well-known theme in Scripture. As an act of judgment on idolatrous Israel, God caused the spiritual eyes and ears of Israel to be closed. They would see (physically) but not perceive (spiritually). God commissioned Isaiah to "shut their eyes; lest they see with their eyes" (Isaiah 6:9-10). Jesus reminded Israel's spiritual leaders of their deafness and blindness—it was the reason they couldn't understand the spiritual importance of His parables (Matthew 13:14-15).

We should not think that spiritual blindness is only an ancient malady. Spiritual seeing comes only through seeking wisdom and discernment (Proverbs 2:1-6). And that calls for humility. God gives grace to the humble but resists the proud (James 4:6). It was the central message of Jesus' parable of the seed, soil, and sower (Matthew 13:1-23). There is great evidence today that the Christian Church is flying blind, as pilots would say. We are operating in physical realms only. When Christians vote with the world on the great moral issues of our day (marriage, abortion, and others), it is plain that we have lost our spiritual perception. We call good evil and evil good—and God says "woe to those" who do so (Isaiah 5:20).

The only salve for such a condition is repentance and submission to the Lord Jesus Christ, asking Him for the fullness and wisdom of His Spirit to restore our spiritual sight.

## *The Prescription for Spiritual Compromise (Revelation 3:19)*

There is only one word of counsel for the spiritually compromised Christian: "Therefore be zealous and repent." But Jesus also puts those firm words in context: "As many as I love, I rebuke and chasten." In spite of their spiritual blindness and nakedness and poverty, Jesus loved the church in Laodicea. And He loves us and the Church around the world that also show signs of being like the church in Laodicea. God doesn't love us only when we are doing the right things. He loves us all the time—and because He does, He wants us to repent when we need to. God loves us too much to leave us the way we are.

If we think "repent" is a harsh message, the message Jesus would be sending if He didn't call us to repentance is even harsher. One commentator explains: "If Jesus did not call people to repentance, he would be sending them a message. Do you know what that message would be? 'Go to Hell.'"[2]

You may be reading these words and realize Jesus is talking to you. You may see yourself in the condition of the church in Laodicea—lukewarm and in spiritual poverty. You may realize that you were "hot" for the Lord when you first became a follower of Christ but now you have cooled off; now you are only lukewarm. What do you do if that describes where you are spiritually? What is the prescription for a compromising Christian and compromising church? One word: repent. Confess your compromise and ask God to forgive you and give you grace to turn in the opposite direction. Ask God to move you from a place of lukewarm compromise to a place of passion for Christ.

## *The Prescription for Their Christlessness (Revelation 3:20-22)*

The last prescription, for their "Christlessness," is in verse 20: "Behold, I stand at the door and knock. If anyone hears My voice and opens the door, I will come in to him and dine with him, and he with Me." This is one of the simplest and most eloquent invitations to salvation and fellowship with God found in all the Bible. It is a picture of Christ seeking entrance to a church which is gained only by His entrance into the hearts of those who make up the Church. He stands at the door and knocks, seeking permission to enter.

It is sad to picture Christ standing outside His own Church, outside a door that is closed not only to Him but to others who might want to enter. It is a picture of a closed, self-absorbed, introverted Church. And as noted throughout this series, from the prophetic perspective, it is the Church of the last days. It is the Church on earth when Christ returns to establish His kingdom. It is a Church too busy with plans and programs and priorities to even notice that Christ has been crowded out. Christ is moved to the margins, then the periphery, and finally He is outside the Church altogether. He is knocking, seeking to be invited back in.

If the Church is to become passionate instead of lukewarm, it will only happen when the Church is rich *in* Him and clothed *with* Him.

Notes:
1. John F. Walvoord, *The Revelation of Jesus Christ* (Chicago, Moody Press, 1966), 94.
2. James M. Hamilton Jr., *Revelation* (Wheaton, IL: Crossway Books, 2012), Kindle edition.

## APPLICATION

1. Why would "The Bereans" be a good name for an adult Sunday school class? (Acts 17:10-12

   a. Were "the Bereans" Christians or Jews? (verses 10-11)

   b. Why did Paul consider the Bereans more "noble-minded" (NASB) than the Jews in Thessalonica? (verse 11)

   c. Why is the phrase "searched the Scriptures daily" a good model for a Christian to follow? How does daily study keep one from becoming lukewarm?

2. What do the following six Scriptures say about Christ as the source of creation?

   a. John 1:1-3

b. Colossians 1:15-17 (What does "firstborn over all creation" mean? What are the implications of all things being created "for Him"?)

c. 1 Corinthians 8:6

d. Hebrews 1:2

e. 1 Peter 1:20

f. James 1:17

3. How does Hebrews 1:3 confirm the fact that Christ is the confirmation of God's Word?

4. How do Paul's words in Romans 12:11 illustrate what the church in Laodicea had not done? (See Revelation 3:15.)

   a. Can you think of another place where Christ used such forceful language as is found in Revelation 3:16? (Peruse Matthew 23 for samples.)

   b. What does such forceful language communicate to us about God's passion?

5. In your opinion, what would characterize a "hot," "lukewarm," or "cold" Christian? What evidence could you observe about each?

   a. Hot/passionate:

   b. Lukewarm:

c. Cold/apathetic

d. How would you characterize yourself?

e. If you don't feel passionate about your Christian life, why not? What could you do to move to the next higher level of commitment?

f. What does/could a passionate church do to keep its members from becoming lukewarm?

6. How can Paul's words in Romans 12:3 address the issue of conceit?

a. What warning does 1 Corinthians 10:12 provide against conceit?

b. What response can a conceited person or church expect from God? (James 4:6)

7. What did God tell Isaiah to tell Israel in Isaiah 6:9-10?

a. How did Jesus use those verses to remind the Jews of their spiritual poverty? (Matthew 13:14-15)

b. What must we do to continually receive insight and discernment from God? (Proverbs 2:1-6

## DID YOU KNOW?

One of the most famous religious paintings in the world was painted by the British artist William Holman Hunt in 1851. The painting is called "The Light of the World." It shows the front of a cottage that is overgrown with vines, the front door closed and shut tight—an image of a neglected and long-closed house. Standing at the door, arrayed in kingly robes with a crown on His head and a lantern in one hand, is Jesus Christ. With His other hand, Christ is knocking on the door hoping to find life within. Someone once accused Holman of a mistake in the painting—he had neglected to paint a handle on the outside of the door. The artist replied that it was not a mistake. There was not meant to be a handle on the outside; the door has to be opened to Christ by those who are within.

# LESSON 9

# A Look Into Heaven

### *Revelation 4:1-11*

*In this lesson we learn what the Church will see upon arriving in heaven just before the Tribulation.*

### OUTLINE

"Heaven" has become a cultural word used by many but understood by few. The book of Revelation gives us the only detailed look into heaven as seen by the apostle John. He used his earthly vocabulary to describe things beyond understanding, yet full of meaning for believers.

I. **The Church's Exit From Earth**
   A. The Sequence of Events in the Book of Revelation
   B. The Silence Concerning the Church in Chapters 4-19
   C. The Spirit of God's Transfer From Earth to Heaven
   D. The Similarities Between Revelation 4:1-2, 1 Corinthians 15, and 1 Thessalonians 4

II. **The Church's Existence in Heaven**
   A. Seated Upon the Throne Is the Triune God
   B. Surrounding the Throne Is a Rainbow
   C. Sitting Around the Throne Are the Twenty-four Elders
   D. Sounding Forth From the Throne Are Lightnings and Thunders and Voices
   E. Spread Before the Throne Is a Sea of Glass
   F. Situated in the Midst of the Throne Are the Four Living Creatures
   G. Singing to the One on the Throne Are the Creatures and the Elders

## OVERVIEW

As mentioned in the previous lesson, the Church is seen only in the first three chapters of Revelation. We have completed our review of the historic and prophetic significance of the seven churches Christ addressed in His letters. Now it is time to look at the Church's relationship to heaven—specifically the Church that will be on earth at the end of this present age prior to the Tribulation. As previously stated, that Church will be removed from earth (Revelation 3:10) and be kept from the trials of the Tribulation, only to then return with Christ to earth at the end of the seven-year period.

# THE CHURCH'S EXIT FROM EARTH

The Rapture of the Church is not mentioned specifically in Revelation but is definitely alluded to. The Church is on earth at the end of Revelation 3 and in heaven at the beginning of Revelation 4. It got there by way of the Rapture.

## The Sequence of Events in the Book of Revelation

Revelation 1:19 is a key verse for understanding the entire book: "Write the things which you have seen, and the things which are, and the things which will take place after this." John is told to write what he will see in three parts. The first section was John's vision of Christ; the second section was the letters to the seven churches.

The third section begins with Revelation 4:1 with the same phrase from Revelation 1:19: "things which must take place after this." "After this" refers to the Church's translation from earth to heaven. John will be recording what will happen on earth "after this." Revelation 2-3 deals with the Church on earth; Revelation 4 forward deals with what happens on earth while the Church is in heaven.

## The Silence Concerning the Church in Chapters 4-19

The word "church" appears 19 times in Revelation 1-3 but not a single time in the rest of the book. (It does occur at the very end of the book [22:16], referring to the vision given to John for "the churches." This is an editorial reference at the end of the book, not an "action" reference.)

Also, the words of Christ to several of the churches—"He who has an ear, let him hear what the Spirit says to the churches"—is modified in Revelation 13:9: "If anyone has an ear, let him hear." No mention is made of "the churches." What John is recording is not for the Church on earth but for whoever reads the vision of the Apocalypse. Beginning with Revelation 4, the Church has been removed from earth.

## *The Spirit of God's Transfer From Earth to Heaven*

In Revelation 2-3 the Holy Spirit is in the midst of the churches, but in Revelation 4:5 we find the Spirit of God in heaven. The Holy Spirit dwells in the Church. When the Church is on earth, the Spirit is on earth; when the Church is in heaven, the Spirit is in heaven. The Spirit will be active during the Tribulation on earth but in more of an Old Testament sense—empowering people and events but not indwelling the Church.

Second Thessalonians 2:7-8 is an important text for understanding the Spirit's role. That passage describes "the mystery of lawlessness" that occurs when "the lawless one is revealed" and "He who now restrains . . . is taken out of the way." The Holy Spirit is "the restrainer" who keeps sin at bay in the world. But once He is removed when the Church is removed, the Antichrist (the "lawless one") will have free reign to unleash hell on earth—literally. If we think life on earth now is chaotic and depraved, it can't compare with what it will be like when the Holy Spirit (the Spirit of *holiness*) is removed.

## *The Similarities Between Revelation 4:1-2, 1 Corinthians 15, and 1 Thessalonians 4*

Three passages of Scripture blend together to give us all the events that will occur at the Rapture.

### A Voice

Revelation 4:1 says John heard a voice beckoning him to heaven. There is a parallel voice in 1 Thessalonians 4:16—the "voice of an archangel" calling the Church from earth at the Rapture.

### A Trumpet

The voice John heard was "like a trumpet" (Revelation 4:1). The same trumpet sound is to be heard at the Rapture (1 Thessalonians 4:16).

**A Change**

John was "immediately ... in the Spirit" (Revelation 4:2). John found himself in a different dimension, a spiritual dimension. The same thing will happen at the resurrection associated with the Rapture: "this corruptible must put on incorruption, and this mortal must put on immortality" (1 Corinthians 15:53).

The voice, trumpet, and change described all indicate a significant shift in orientation that occurs at the Rapture. I take a pretribulational view of the Rapture, meaning the Church will leave earth *before* the Tribulation begins. The blending of important passages from Revelation, 1 Corinthians, 1 Thessalonians, and others support that view. Revelation 4–19 covers the seven years of trial that will come upon the earth. But the Church—all true believers in Christ—will be kept from that hour (Revelation 3:10).

# THE CHURCH'S EXISTENCE IN HEAVEN (REVELATION 4:1-11)

Again: Revelation 1–3, the Church is on earth; Revelation 4–19, the Church is in heaven. It is through "a door standing open in heaven" that John gains access to what he records (Revelation 4:1). This door is opened again in Revelation 19:11 and Christ comes through it, followed by the armies of heaven, as He returns to earth at the end of the Tribulation. The door opens first for John to go up and in, and second for Christ to come through and down to earth.

"Throne" is a key word in Revelation, occurring dozens of times beginning in Revelation 1:4 and ending in Revelation 22:3. Throne is a symbol of sovereignty and authority—God's in this case. God's sovereignty over the earth is one of the great themes of Revelation. John's vision of heaven includes the prominent position of God's throne. Regardless of how chaotic things on earth can get, God is ruling over all (Psalm 9:7-8; 103:19).

It is this very throne of God we are encouraged to come before to find grace and mercy in time of need (Hebrews 4:16). Beginning in Revelation 4, the age of grace and mercy is over. The throne in heaven is a throne of judgment that decrees great trials of judgment on earth during the Tribulation. That is the picture we get from Revelation 4–19. Everything that happens in the rest of Revelation is based on the centrality of God's throne in heaven.

## Seated Upon the Throne Is the Triune God (Revelation 4:2-3a)

"And He who sat [on the throne] was like a jasper and a sardius stone in appearance" (verse 3; 3:21). Neither jasper nor sardius are mentioned elsewhere in Scripture, but we know they were precious stones. Their mention here is to ascribe radiance and worth to the Father who is on the throne. God has no physical appearance (John 4:24), so can only be described in terms of visual radiance.

## Surrounding the Throne Is a Rainbow (Revelation 4:3b)

"And there was a rainbow around the throne, in appearance like an emerald." The rainbow was a reminder of the rainbow in Genesis that meant God would never again judge the earth with a flood. The rainbow around God's throne is a reminder that He is a covenant-keeping God.

## Sitting Around the Throne Are the Twenty-four Elders (Revelation 4:4)

Around the throne John saw "twenty-four thrones" with "twenty-four elders sitting on them. The elders were "clothed in white robes" and had "crowns of gold" on their heads. These elders represent the Church, the saints who followed Jesus Christ. We know this for three reasons.

1. By the Praise on Their Lips (Revelation 5:8-10)

In Revelation 5:8-10 we "hear" what the elders are singing as praise: "For You were slain, and have redeemed us to God by Your blood out of every tribe and tongue and people and nation." They say more than that, but those are the words that identify who they represent: believers in Jesus Christ. The twenty-four elders represent the Church. The elders also declare that they "shall reign on the earth." The Church will one day rule with Christ during the Millennium. Revelation 17:14 and 19:14 describe Christ's followers returning with Him when He judges the enemies of God at the end of the Tribulation, then reigning with Him during the Millennium.

2. By the Clothes on Their Bodies (Revelation 4:4b)

The elders are clothed in "white robes." The saints that return from heaven with Christ will be dressed "in fine linen, clean and bright, for the fine linen is the righteous acts of the saints" (Revelation 19:8).

Those returning with Christ are "His wife," the Bride of Christ (Revelation 19:7). The elders and saints are arrayed in white linen and represent the Church in heaven during the Tribulation.

3. By the Crowns Upon Their Heads (Revelation 4:4c)

The elders were wearing "crowns of gold on their heads." The word here for crown is not the Greek word for a diadem, the crown of a ruler. Rather, it is the word for the crown worn by a victor, like the champions in the Greek and Roman games. So the elders are not rulers, they are victors. Only the Church has been judged and rewarded at this point (at the Judgment Seat of Christ—Romans 14:10; 1 Corinthians 3:11-15; 2 Corinthians 5:10). Old Testament saints will not be judged until the Second Coming. So these "crowned" elders can represent none other than the Church. They represent all who have believed in Christ and will participate in the Rapture and be in heaven during the Tribulation.

The Church was promised a throne, crowns, and white garments in Christ's letters to the churches (Revelation 2:10; 3:18, 21). And the twenty-four elders have all three.

## Sounding Forth From the Throne Are Lightnings and Thunders and Voices (Revelation 4:5)

"And from the throne proceeded lightnings, thunderings, and voices." This is reminiscent of the sights and sounds at Mount Sinai when Moses received the law from God (Exodus 19:16). These displays represent the awesomeness of God in giving the Law and then in the judgment that will come from humanity having broken His laws. Again, God's throne in Revelation 4–19 is a throne of judgment, not of grace, as seen in Revelation 8:5; 11:19; 16:18.

There will be cataclysmic events during the Tribulation worse than anything in human history, all as judgments upon an earth that has rejected Him. When John saw God's throne and the awesome sights and sounds coming from it, he knew judgment was coming for earth. But He also saw the twenty-four elders (the Church) gathered safely around the throne.

## Spread Before the Throne Is a Sea of Glass (Revelation 4:6a)

Before the throne of God John saw "a sea of glass, like crystal." We don't know exactly what that means, but it is similar to what Moses, Aaron, and the 70 elders of Israel saw as they approached

God: "And there was under His feet as it were a paved work of sapphire stone, and it was like the very heavens in its clarity" (Exodus 24:10).

The picture of the throne room of heaven is expanding: the throne, the rainbow, thunder, lightning, 24 elders around the throne, and a "sea of glass" before the throne. It is possible that this "glass" is the same material and appearance as mentioned in Revelation 21:21: "the street of the [New Jerusalem] was pure gold, like transparent glass." The "gold" in heaven is not the same as gold on earth; our gold is obviously not "like transparent glass." There is going to be something uniquely valuable about the construction materials in the New Jerusalem—materials which would dazzle us now if we could see them. John was obviously using whatever earthly metaphors available in his vocabulary to describe what he was seeing—like the gates of the city each being made of "one pearl" (Revelation 21:21). We have never seen a gate-sized pearl on earth, but we will in heaven!

## *Situated in the Midst of the Throne Are the Four Living Creatures (Revelation 4:6b-8)*

The image of the throne room gets even more complex with John's description of "four living creatures full of eyes in front and in back" around the throne (verse 6b). He gives detailed descriptions of the creatures in verses 7-8. The four creatures Ezekiel saw were somewhat different from the ones John saw, but Ezekiel goes on to tell us what they represent in Ezekiel 10:14-15. One had the appearance of a cherub, one a man, one a lion, and one an eagle. And he calls them all "cherubim." So all were angels!

I believe that is what the four creatures John saw were as well—angels of God who were about to be dispatched to carry out the judgments of God on the earth. When God begins releasing judgments on the earth it is the four living creatures who are the agents of judgment (Revelation 6:1, 3, 5, 7). They are standing in the throne room of God waiting for their assignments to release the white, red, black, and pale horses of judgment upon the earth (Revelation 6:1-8).

## *Singing to the One on the Throne Are the Creatures and the Elders (Revelation 4:9-11)*

In addition to facilitating judgment on earth during the Tribulation, the four living creatures lead in worship in heaven! Their worship of "glory and honor and thanks to God" causes the 24 elders to "fall down before Him who sits on the throne and worship Him." The elders "cast their crowns before the throne" addressing God directly: "You are worthy, O Lord, to receive glory and honor and power; for You created all things, and by Your will they exist and were created."

This is a heavenly choir that John sees through the door in heaven that has been opened to him. God is about to judge the earth, but before doing so the living creatures point out that it was God who created it. There is nothing in the creation of God that inherently deserves judgment. Rather it is that man has defiled the creation through sin.

In the midst of the thunder and lightning and sounds emanating from the throne come the voices of the living creatures in praise to God. We can only imagine what such a scene looked like when John saw it. It is amazing to realize that the elders—the Church—take the crowns of faithfulness they have received and lay them at the base of the throne as an offering of reverence and worship. It was a way of saying, "It was your faithfulness to us that allowed us to be faithful to You." It is only by grace through faith that we have been saved—and even that faith "is the gift of God" (Ephesians 2:8-9). If we have had faith in Jesus Christ, it is only by the grace-gift of God that we were able to do so. Thus returning our rewards to Him in response to His grace to us is entirely appropriate.

We don't talk a lot about rewards in the Church today, but we should. I don't want to be empty-handed when it comes time to worship the Lord in heaven. I want to have something to lay at the foot of the throne of God in thanks for what Christ has done for me. And the only way to gain those rewards is to live faithfully as His follower. It's one thing to be saved; it's another thing to be saved and be blessed with a crown at the Judgment Seat of Christ that we can then offer up to God in thanksgiving.

The elders praise God speaking directly to Him (verse 11) as opposed to the living creatures' words of praise (verse 8). Why? Because the living creatures were never saved by the blood of the Lamb like the elders were (1 Peter 1:12). Those who have been saved from sin don't sing praises *about* God; they sing praises *to* God. When we worship Him, we know the value of the blood of Christ personally. We should praise Him in second-person terms: "*You* are worthy, O Lord."

Can you praise the Lord that way, in personal terms? If not, accept Him as *your* Lord and Savior today, talking *to* Him and not just *about* Him.

## APPLICATION

1. Review from Lesson 7: What promise did Christ make to the church in Philadelphia? (Revelation 3:10)

    a. From a prophetic perspective, how does that promise apply to the universal Church?

    b. Where will the Church be during the coming seven-year Tribulation?

    c. From this lesson: Describe the change in John's perspective between the end of Revelation 3 and the beginning of Revelation 4. How does Revelation 1:19 help you understand this change in perspective?

*A Look Into Heaven* • 121

d. Describe the three vantage points of Revelation 1:19. What does each represent?

• Things you have seen:

• Things which are:

• Things which will take place after this:

e. In Revelation 2-3 the Church was on _____, while in Revelation 4-19 the Church is in_____.

f. The word "_____" doesn't occur in Revelation after chapter 3. Why is this?

g. Compare Revelation 1:11 with Revelation 13:9. How and why are they different?

2. Read 2 Thessalonians 2:7-10.

   a. How do 1 John 4:3 and 1 John 5:9 help explain the "mystery of lawlessness"? (verse 7)

   b. Who or what is restraining that lawlessness in the world today? (verse 7)

   c. How will that "restraint" be taken "out of the way"? (verse 7)

   d. Where does the Holy Spirit principally reside on earth today? (1 Corinthians 6:19)

e. When the Church is raptured from earth, what will that mean regarding the Holy Spirit's presence on earth?

f. Who is "the lawless one"? Who will empower him? (verses 8-10; 1 John 2:18)

3. How is the phrase "Come up here" a synonym for the Rapture of the Church? (Revelation 4:1)

4. What is the difference between how the living creatures praised God (Revelation 4:8) and the way the elders praised Him (Revelation 4:11)?

a. What had the elders experienced that the angelic creatures had never experienced?

b. Why is "you" (second person language) a more intimate form than "he" (third person language)?

c. Which do you tend to use more?

d. Why did the elders cast their crowns before the throne? Why was it appropriate? (Revelation 4:10)

---

**DID YOU KNOW?**

A "throne" is mentioned 159 times in Scripture—not a surprise since the Bible is the story of God's throne (kingdom) vanquishing all competing thrones from earth. In Israel, as well as competing religions, the earthly throne was to be a mirror of the heavenly throne. God's will and authority were vested in His earthly king and the throne on which the king sat was the symbol of that divine-human chain of authority. John establishes the point early in his vision that God's throne is occupied by the One "who was and is and is to come!" (Revelation 4:8; see also 1:4, 8). This description is an expanded paraphrase of the sovereign name of God given by Him to Moses: "I am" (Exodus 3:14-15)—the ultimate statement of sovereign authority.

# ADDITIONAL RESOURCES
## BY DR. DAVID JEREMIAH

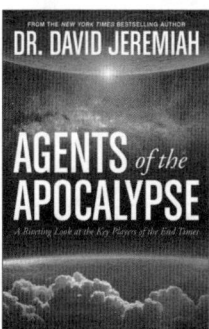

### AGENTS OF THE APOCALYPSE
Dr. David Jeremiah explores Revelation's major players in *Agents of the Apocalypse.* From the exile and the martyrs to the dragon and the King, these key individuals and groups will populate the world at the end of the age. In each chapter of this book, Dr. Jeremiah provides fictional, Bible-based stories about the end-time players and backs up each with "the Scripture behind the story" to help us understand what the end times means for us today.

### ESCAPE THE COMING NIGHT
Tragedy and chaos surround us—violence and corruption occur every day. So how can we explain the troubling circumstances? Is it really possible to find peace amidst the problems? In *Escape the Coming Night,* Dr. David Jeremiah narrates the book of Revelation and answers challenging questions like these in order for us to see what God declares about the signs, symbols, and prophecies of the end times.

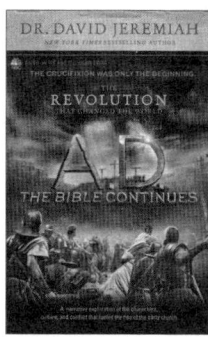

## A.D. THE REVOLUTION THAT CHANGED THE WORLD

In *A.D. The Revolution That Changed the World*, Dr. David Jeremiah takes us on a voyage through the life of the apostles after Christ's resurrection. Following the life of Stephen, Paul, Peter, and others, Dr. Jeremiah shows us that these apostles not only shared the Good News but continued to fight for their faith despite persecution, adversity, and rebellion. This book holds within it the action-packed struggles and successes that led to the formation of the early church.

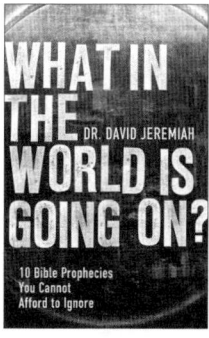

## WHAT IN THE WORLD IS GOING ON?

Many theories about the end times abound in our world today. There are hundreds of books predicting the future, but there is no other prophecy book like this one. In *What in the World Is Going On?* Dr. David Jeremiah identifies the ten most important prophecies of the Bible to help us understand the mysteries of the end times. This eye-opening book is an essential read in this world filled with confusing theories and false prophecies.

---

Each of these resources was created from a teaching series by Dr. David Jeremiah. For more information about correlating materials contact Turning Point

For pricing information and ordering, contact us at

P.O. Box 3838
San Diego, CA 92163
(800) 947-1993
WWW.DAVIDJEREMIAH.ORG

# STAY CONNECTED
## TO DR. DAVID JEREMIAH

Take advantage of two great ways to let Dr. David Jeremiah give you spiritual direction every day! Both are absolutely FREE.

### *Turning Points* Magazine and Devotional

Receive Dr. David Jeremiah's magazine, *Turning Points* each month:

- Thematic study focus
- 48 pages of life-changing reading
- Relevant articles
- Special features
- Daily devotional readings
- Bible study resource offers
- Live event schedule
- Radio & television information

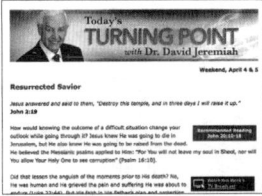

### Daily Turning Point E-Devotional

Start your day off right! Find words of inspiration and spiritual motivation waiting for you on your computer every morning! Receive a daily e-devotion communication from David Jeremiah that will strengthen your walk with God and encourage you to live the authentic Christian life.

---

There are two easy ways to sign up for these free resources from Turning Point. Visit us online at www.DavidJeremiah.org and select "Subscribe to Daily Devotional by Email" or visit the home page and find Daily Devotional to subscribe to your monthly copy of *Turning Points*.